✧ *Companions for the Journey* ✧

Praying with
Thomas Aquinas

✧ *Companions for the Journey* ✧

Praying with Thomas Aquinas

by
Mary Mercy Houle, OP
Michael Monshau, OP
and
Patrick Norris, OP

Saint Mary's Press
Christian Brothers Publications
Winona, Minnesota

With love and appreciation
to our own companions for the journey,
the brothers and sisters of our Dominican communities:
the Cloistered Nuns
of the Monastery of the Blessed Sacrament,
Farmington Hills, Michigan,
and the Friars Preachers
of the Chicago Province of Saint Albert the Great

Genuine recycled paper with 10% post-consumer waste.
Printed with soy-based ink.

The publishing team for this book included Michael Wilt, development editor; Cheryl Drivdahl, copy editor; Brooke E. Saron, production editor; Hollace Storkel, typesetter; Laurie Geisler, cover designer; Sam Thiewes, illustrator; pre-press, printing, and binding by the graphics division of Saint Mary's Press.

The acknowledgments continue on page 123.

Printed in the United States of America

Printing: 9 8 7 6 5 4 3 2 1

Year: 2008 07 06 05 04 03 02 01 00

ISBN 0-88489-561-0

✧ Contents ✧

Foreword   7

Preface   13

A Note on the *Summa Theologiae*   15

Introduction   16

Meditations

  1. **The Trinity**   *31*

  2. **The Goodness of Creation**   *37*

  3. **God's Unconditional Love**   *44*

  4. **Happiness**   *49*

  5. **Our Response to the Divine Call**   *55*

  6. **Friendship with God**   *61*

  7. **Virtue**   *67*

  8. **The Gifts of the Holy Spirit**   *73*

  9. **Corpus Christi**   *80*

10. **Petitionary Prayer**   *85*

11. **The Pater Noster**   *90*

12. **Truth**   *96*

13. **Study**   *102*

14. **Preaching**   *109*

15. **"Nothing but You, O Lord!"**   *115*

Works Cited   *120*

For Further Reading   *122*

✧ Foreword ✧

Companions for the Journey

Just as food is required for human life, so are companions. Indeed, the word *companions* comes from two Latin words: *com,* meaning "with," and *panis,* meaning "bread." Companions nourish our heart, mind, soul, and body. They are also the people with whom we can celebrate the sharing of bread.

Perhaps the most touching stories in the Bible are about companionship: the Last Supper, the wedding feast at Cana, the sharing of the loaves and the fishes, and Jesus' breaking of bread with the disciples on the road to Emmaus. Each incident of companionship with Jesus revealed more about his mercy, love, wisdom, suffering, and hope. When Jesus went to pray in the Garden of Olives, he craved the companionship of the Apostles. They let him down. But God sent the Spirit to inflame the hearts of the Apostles, and they became faithful companions to Jesus and to one another.

Throughout history, other faithful companions have followed Jesus and the Apostles. These saints and mystics have also taken the journey from conversion, through suffering, to resurrection. Just as they were inspired by the holy people who went before them, so too may you be inspired by these saints and mystics and take them as your companions on your spiritual journey.

The Companions for the Journey series is a response to the spiritual hunger of Christians. This series makes available the rich spiritual teachings of mystics and guides whose wisdom can help us on our pilgrimage. As you complete the last meditation in each volume, it is hoped that you will feel supported, challenged, and affirmed by a soul-companion on your spiritual journey.

The spiritual hunger that has emerged over the last twenty years is a great sign of renewal in Christian life. People fill retreat programs and workshops on topics in spirituality. The demand for spiritual directors exceeds the number available. Interest in the lives and writings of saints and mystics is increasing as people search for models of whole and holy Christian life.

Praying with Thomas Aquinas

Praying with Thomas Aquinas is more than just a book about the spirituality of Thomas Aquinas. This book seeks to engage you in praying in the way that Thomas did about issues and themes that were central to his experience. Each meditation can enlighten your understanding of his spirituality and lead you to reflect on your own experience.

The goal of *Praying with Thomas Aquinas* is that you will discover Thomas's rich spirituality and integrate his spirit and wisdom into your relationship with God, with your brothers and sisters, and with your own heart and mind.

Suggestions for Praying with Thomas Aquinas

Meet Thomas Aquinas, a fascinating companion for your pilgrimage, by reading the introduction to this book. It provides a brief biography of Thomas and an outline of the major themes of his spirituality.

Once you meet Thomas Aquinas, you will be ready to pray with him and to encounter God, your sisters and brothers, and yourself in new and wonderful ways. To help your prayer, here are some suggestions that have been part of the tradition of Christian spirituality:

Create a sacred space. Jesus said, "Whenever you pray, go into your room and shut the door and pray to your [God] who is in secret; and your [God] who sees in secret will reward you" (Matthew 6:6). Solitary prayer is best done in a place where you can have privacy and silence, both of which can be luxuries in the life of busy people. If privacy and silence are not possible, create a quiet, safe place within yourself, perhaps while riding to and from work, while sitting in line at the dentist's office, or while waiting for someone. Do the best you can, knowing that a loving God is present everywhere. Whether the meditations in this book are used for solitary prayer or with a group, try to create a prayerful mood with candles, meditative music, an open Bible, or a crucifix.

Open yourself to the power of prayer. Every human experience has a religious dimension. All of life is suffused with God's presence. So remind yourself that God is present as you begin your period of prayer. Do not worry about distractions. If something keeps intruding during your prayer, spend some time talking with God about it. Be flexible because God's spirit blows where it will.

Prayer can open your mind and widen your vision. Be open to new ways of seeing God, people, and yourself. As you open yourself to the spirit of God, different emotions are evoked, such as sadness from tender memories, or joy from a celebration recalled. Our emotions are messages from God that can tell us much about our spiritual quest. Also, prayer strengthens our will to act. Through prayer, God can touch our will and empower us to live according to what we know is true.

Finally, many of the meditations in this book will call you to employ your memories, your imagination, and the circumstances of your life as subjects for prayer. The great mystics and saints realized that they had to use all their resources to know God better. Indeed, God speaks to us continually and touches us constantly. We must learn to listen and feel with all the means that God has given us.

Come to prayer with an open mind, heart, and will.

Preview each meditation before beginning. After you have placed yourself in God's presence, spend a few moments previewing the readings and especially the reflection activities. Several reflection activities are given in each meditation because different styles of prayer appeal to different personalities or personal needs. **Note that each meditation has more reflection activities than can be done during one prayer period. Therefore, select only one or two reflection activities each time you use a meditation. Do not feel compelled to complete all the reflection activities.**

Read meditatively. Each meditation offers you a story about Thomas Aquinas and a reading from his writings. Take your time reading. If a particular phrase touches you, stay with it. Relish its feelings, meanings, and concerns.

Use the reflections. Following the readings is a short reflection in commentary form, which is meant to give perspective to the readings. Then you are offered several ways of meditating on the readings and the theme of the prayer. You may be familiar with the different methods of meditating, but in case you are not, they are described briefly here:

✦ *Repeated short prayer or mantra:* One means of focusing your prayer is to use a *mantra,* or "prayer word." The mantra may be a single word or a short phrase taken from the readings or from the Scriptures. For example, a short prayer for meditation 13 in this book might simply be "I am here, God." Repeated slowly in harmony with your breathing, the mantra helps you center your heart and mind on one action or attribute of God.

✦ *Lectio divina:* This type of meditation is "divine studying," a concentrated reflection on the word of God or the wisdom of a spiritual writer. Most often in *lectio divina,* you will be invited to read one of the passages several times and then concentrate on one or two sentences, pondering their meaning for you and their effect on you. *Lectio divina* commonly ends with formulation of a resolution.

✦ *Guided meditation:* In this type of meditation, our imagination helps us consider alternative actions and likely consequences. Our imagination helps us experience new ways of seeing God, our neighbors, ourselves, and nature. When Jesus told his followers parables and stories, he engaged their imagination. In this book, you will be invited to follow guided meditations.

One way of doing a guided meditation is to read the scene or story several times, until you know the outline and can recall it when you enter into reflection. Or before your prayer time, you may wish to record the meditation on a tape recorder. If so, remember to allow pauses for reflection between phrases and to speak with a slow, peaceful pace and tone. Then, during prayer, when you have finished the readings and the reflection commentary, you can turn on your recording of the meditation and be led through it. If you find your own voice too distracting, ask a friend to make the tape for you.

✦ *Examen of consciousness:* The reflections often will ask you to examine how God has been speaking to you in your past and present experience—in other words, the reflections will ask you to examine your awareness of God's presence in your life.

✦ *Journal writing:* Writing is a process of discovery. If you write for any length of time, stating honestly what is on your mind and in your heart, you will unearth much about who you are, how you stand with your God, what deep longings reside in your soul, and more. In some reflections, you will be asked to write a dialog with Jesus or someone else. If you have never used writing as a means of meditation, try it. Reserve a special notebook for your journal writing. If desired, you can go back to your entries at a future time for an examen of consciousness.

✦ *Action:* Occasionally, a reflection will suggest singing a favorite hymn, going out for a walk, or undertaking some other physical activity. Actions can be meaningful forms of prayer.

Using the Meditations for Group Prayer

If you wish to use the meditations for community prayer, these suggestions may help:

✦ Read the theme to the group. Call the community into the presence of God, using the short opening prayer. Invite one or two participants to read one or both readings. If you use both readings, observe the pause between them.

✦ The reflection commentary may be used as a reading, or it can be deleted, depending on the needs and interests of the group.

✦ Select one of the reflection activities for your group. Allow sufficient time for your group to reflect, to recite a centering prayer or mantra, to accomplish a studying prayer (*lectio divina*), or to finish an examen of consciousness. Depending on the group and the amount of available time, you may want to invite the participants to share their reflections, responses, or petitions with the group.

✦ Reading the passage from the Scriptures may serve as a summary of the meditation.

✦ If a formulated prayer or a psalm is given as a closing, it may be recited by the entire group. Or you may ask participants to offer their own prayers for the closing.

Now you are ready to begin praying with Thomas Aquinas, a faithful and caring companion on this stage of your spiritual journey. It is hoped that you will find him to be a true soul-companion.

CARL KOCH
Series Editor

✧ Preface ✧

When Saint Dominic founded the Holy Preaching in the early thirteenth century, he invited men and women to enter into a collaborative effort to preach the Gospel of Jesus Christ. This preaching movement (which would become more commonly known as the Order of Preachers or the Dominicans) was collaborative because at its outset, its membership included ordained and nonordained friars and contemplative nuns. Eventually, active religious sisters, laypeople, secular institutes, and diocesan priests would also be part of the Dominican family. Members of the order quickly discovered that their preaching mission would extend well beyond liturgical homiletic preaching and would include research and writing, teaching, spiritual direction, foreign mission activity, monastic contemplation, and pastoring. The authoring of *Praying with Thomas Aquinas* has been yet another satisfying experience of collaborative Dominican preaching. We three Dominicans—a cloistered nun and a friar priest in metropolitan Detroit, and another friar priest in Saint Louis—have grown in our relationship with our brother Thomas as a result of turning again to his great works, recalling his context, and applying both to contemporary spirituality. Because God, as revealed in Jesus Christ, was the passion and the subject of the lifework of Thomas, we recognize the publication of this volume on prayer in the spirit of the Angelic Doctor as one more expression of our order's mission of preaching the Gospel.

Numerous people supported and assisted us as we engaged this project, and we wish to thank them here. Fr. Benedict Ashley, OP, Fr. Michael Mascari, OP, Fr. Matthew Rzeczkowski, OP, Dr. Steven Snyder, and Fr. Dennis Zusy, OP, examined the early plans for this book and offered helpful suggestions as well as encouragement. Ms. Charlotte Ruzicka generously responded to the developing manuscript and provided secretarial assistance. Sr. Catherine Mary Coughlin, OP, was wonderfully generous in applying her mastery of the computer and electronic mail processes, to ensure that three coauthors separated by hundreds of miles remained current with one another's work. Our series editor, Carl Koch of Saint Mary's Press, showed much patience while providing critical editorial direction. Our religious superiors, Sr. Mary Thomas Michalek, OP, and Fr. Edward Ruane, OP, with whose permission we presented this work for publication, were supportive and gracious. To all of these wonderful people who have contributed in their various ways to the completion of *Praying with Thomas Aquinas,* we are most grateful. In a special way, we feel gratitude to our holy father, Saint Dominic, whose own response to the Gospel brought our cherished Dominican order into existence. Indeed, it is through our shared experience with Thomas as children of Saint Dominic that we find our greatest affiliation with Thomas himself.

In a significant way, we have enjoyed the support of our Dominican communities, the Cloistered Nuns of the Monastery of the Blessed Sacrament in Farmington Hills, Michigan, and the Friars Preachers of the Chicago Province of Saint Albert the Great. Our sisters and brothers have nurtured our Dominican vocations and provided lifelong opportunities for study and learning, and it is to them that we dedicate *Praying with Thomas Aquinas.*

M.M.H.
M.J.M.
P.F.N.

✧ A Note on the ✧
Summma Theologiae

Unless otherwise noted, quotations from the *Summa Theologiae* of Thomas Aquinas are taken from the 1964–1975 edition, published in sixty volumes, by Blackfriars (see "Works Cited" for bibliographic details). The *Summa Theologiae* is divided into three parts (I; I-II, II-II; and III). Each part consists of numbered questions, and each question is answered in a series of articles. Hence, the citation *Summa* I, 38, 2, refers to part I, question 38, article 2. (The articles are further broken down into objections and Thomas's numbered answers to those objections. For the purposes of this book, we have limited the citations as described.)

✧ Introduction ✧

In the 1998 encyclical *Faith and Reason (Fides et Ratio)*, Pope John Paul II devotes a major section to Saint Thomas Aquinas. Noting Thomas's ability to integrate faith and reason in a proper fashion, the pope comments, "This is why the church has been justified in consistently proposing St. Thomas as a master of thought and a model of the right way to do theology" (no. 43). The pope's words reinforce the commonly held notion that Aquinas was an intellectual giant whose brilliance has been immortalized through the use of his great theological work the *Summa Theologiae.*

Viewed in that light, Aquinas seems an unlikely companion on the way of prayer and spirituality. Most readers probably would not initially suppose that Thomas was an eminently practical spiritual theologian as well as a man of profound and affective prayer. Yet he was. He is a saint of the church not because of his brilliant theology but because his theology, poetry, hymns, and life itself expressed and flowed from an abiding and holy relationship with God. Today, more than ever, the spirituality of Thomas has much to offer the clergy, religious, and laypeople who seek to deepen their spirituality, especially their life of prayer.

Thomas's Early Years

Thomas was born in Roccasecca in southern Italy, close to Monte Cassino and Naples, scholars believe in 1224 or 1225. He seems to have been one of five boys and ten children born to Landulf and Theodora, in a devout family of the lower nobility. Because he was the youngest boy, his parents destined him for religious life, anticipating that he would become the Benedictine abbot at Monte Cassino. From his earliest childhood, Thomas himself gave signs that he was destined for service to God in the church. Legend has it that as an infant, he picked up a scrap of parchment off the ground and, as most children do, immediately shoved it into his mouth. When his nurse finally retrieved the parchment from the wailing Thomas, she noted that it bore the words "Ave Maria." And on several occasions as a young student in the Benedictine school, Thomas seemed fascinated by the question, What is God?

Thomas was educated by the Benedictines and became steeped in their rich liturgical tradition. He was sent to the University of Naples for additional studies in 1239, and it seemed that he was well on his way to becoming a Benedictine. But during his years of study in Naples, two influences radically reshaped his future. First, in Naples, he encountered members of a relatively new religious group given to living the apostolic life and preaching the good news of salvation as mendicants (who held everything in common and begged for their daily food). These white-habited brothers of the Order of Friars Preachers (the Dominicans) intrigued Thomas. They integrated many elements of monastic life, such as wearing habits and chanting the Office in chorus, with a mission in the world: To preach and teach for the sake of the salvation of souls through a strong intellectual life and a dedication to apostolic poverty. Second, at the University of Naples, his teachers introduced Thomas to the writings of the Greek philosopher Aristotle, whose works were forbidden in Catholic schools at the time.

Beginning the Dominican Journey

Inspired by the Dominican way of life, and with a tremendous intellectual curiosity about how Aristotle could enhance his understanding of the Catholic faith, Thomas joined the Dominicans in April 1244. In so doing, he abandoned his parents' lifelong plan for him to join the Benedictines at Monte Cassino, who were noble, wealthy, and established. His father had died in 1243, but his mother was still very much alive. Although

Theodora was no doubt delighted by her son's decision to enter religious life, she was against his entering the mendicant, cash-poor, upstart Order of Preachers, and she took forceful steps that made her opposition clear.

While on the way from Rome to Paris with some of his Dominican brothers, Thomas was kidnapped, on Theodora's orders, and detained in the tower of the family castle in Montesangiovanni. There is strong evidence, and not merely pious legend, that his family procured the services of a prostitute to try to tempt the young friar, and that Thomas drove the woman from the room. Less certain historically is a report that Thomas was visited by angels who gave him an angelic cord for his waist as a weapon against future temptations against chastity. However, there is no doubt that Thomas lived out the virtue of chastity. Soon after the kidnapping, he was moved to the family home. There, he remained under virtual house arrest for over a year, subjected to his family's pleadings to change his mind. They even offered to arrange for Thomas to be abbot at Monte Cassino while wearing the Dominican habit. Thomas remained resolute. In fact, rather than altering his course, Thomas convinced his sister to become a nun. Sensing the impossibility of changing the iron-willed Thomas, the family allowed him to return to the Dominicans in the summer of 1245.

Although scholars are unsure, it is likely that at this time Thomas went to the Dominican community in Paris, where he studied with Albert the Great (another Dominican and a master of theology). In 1248, he moved with Albert to Cologne and the German *studium.* His fellow students nicknamed Thomas the Dumb Ox because of his quiet, unassuming, and humble nature, coupled with his great height and size. But Albert recognized the intellectual potential of young Thomas and is said to have noted, "We call him the Dumb Ox, but the bellowing of that ox will resound throughout the whole world" (Weisheipl, p. 45). Thomas was ordained a priest in 1250 or 1251. The Dominican leadership asked him to return to Paris in 1252 to study to be a master of theology. Because of his youth, Thomas was reticent and apprehensive about this next step, but with trust in God and his usual vigor, he embraced his studies and flourished.

In 1256, still in France, Thomas became embroiled in the anti-mendicant controversy. The secular theologians at the University of Paris resented the presence of the Dominicans and Franciscans because of their popularity, their holiness of life, their role as strikebreakers at the university years earlier, their theological positions, and their success in drawing revenue away from the secular priests, who were not affiliated with religious orders. Thomas, Albert the Great, and Bonaventure (a Franciscan) defended the mendicant way of life. It is unclear how much Thomas helped to quell the controversy, but he did write a paper defending his order; that paper remains one of the most eloquent and succinct defenses of the mendicant movement.

Thomas the Master of Sacred Theology

After being accepted as a master of sacred theology, Thomas prospered, lecturing on the Scriptures and involving himself with the disputed questions of the day. He produced several commentaries on the Scriptures and began work on a text whose purpose, in part, was to help missionaries in Muslim territories. Designed not to prove the Catholic faith but to show that the Catholic faith was not unreasonable, that text set a tone for the integration of philosophy and theology for years to come. Thomas also became known as a great preacher. His homilies moved people to weep and to cheer. The great intellectual giant was also a powerful evangelizer, very much attuned to the Dominican mission.

Thomas left Paris in 1259, and for the next ten years taught and wrote in various Italian cities, including Rome. Pope Urban IV enlisted his help to deal with questions concerning the Greek church and to write the liturgical texts for the feast of Corpus Christi. Several times during this period, Thomas turned down an offer to be a cardinal, choosing instead to serve the Dominicans as a teacher and as preacher general. Later, he would turn down the opportunity to be archbishop of Naples. Thomas always preferred the gift of wisdom to all other honors.

While Thomas was in Italy, his preaching was so impressive that he was invited to deliver a sermon at Saint Peter's in Rome during Lent. Also during this time, he began his great work the *Summa Theologiae*. Although modern students might find it hard to believe, the *Summa* was designed for beginners in theology. Thomas saw a need for an organized, nonverbose, nonrepetitious introduction to sacred doctrine. Throughout these years, the pace of his written work accelerated. He often kept four scribes busy simultaneously; legend has it that his powers of concentration were so superb that he could dictate in his sleep.

By 1269, the Dominicans had requested that Thomas move back to the University of Paris to reclaim his chair in theology. A second wave of anti-mendicant feelings had emerged. Obedient as always, Thomas went to Paris and again wrote and debated in support of the Franciscans and Dominicans. He also tried to stem the tide of misinterpretations of Aristotle that had crept into the work of scholars in Paris. Ironically, his own use of Aristotle would lead others to view Thomas's work with suspicion.

Thomas lectured in Paris for only three years before returning to Naples in 1272. There, he continued to produce at an incredible pace. At times modifying or sometimes even changing ideas from his previous work, Thomas showed his synthetic brilliance but also his heart. In the last part of the *Summa,* a much more affective Thomas emerges, less distant, less abstract. Throughout his life, Thomas was given over to tears of pleading, and tears of joy when celebrating Mass. When confounded by a question, he would place his head against the tabernacle and beg in tears for wisdom from the One who is Wisdom. As his work in theology and his prayer led him deeper into the mystery of the Godhead, Thomas slept and ate less and less and worked more and more.

An Untimely Death

This excessive routine took its toll. On 6 December 1273, the feast of Saint Nicholas, Thomas announced that he could no longer write. To his good friend, scribe, and confessor Reginald of Piperno, he uttered that he could not go on "because all that I have written seems like straw to me" (Weisheipl, p. 321). It is not known exactly what happened. Did he have a mental or physical breakdown from overwork? Had he suffered a type of stroke? Whatever the physical reality, there is speculation that it was accompanied by a profound spiritual vision and ecstasy that made his written work seem less important to him. Although his work clearly *was* important, Thomas's experience is a profound reminder of just how much the eye has not seen, nor the ear heard, what awaits us.

Soon after, Pope Gregory X called Thomas as an advisor to the Council of Lyons in France. On the way there, in February 1274, Thomas hit his head on a low-hanging branch. He did not seem to be seriously injured, and stopped at Maenza to visit his niece, but his condition started to deteriorate. As he grew more and more ill, he asked to be moved to the Cistercian Abbey at nearby Fossanova. There, he gradually declined, and having received the sacraments, died in peace on 7 March 1274.

Thomas the Man

So ended the life of a man who had given himself to God. Thomas had been both literally and figuratively a giant of his age. Standing well over six feet tall, he towered above most people, and he was well built (though he was not obese, as he is sometimes portrayed; his austerity and thousands of miles trudged by foot over Europe prevented that). He was also an unparalleled intellectual giant, and his reputation in that regard is probably most prevalent today. Yet his great intellect did not lessen but enhanced his profound humanity. Thomas was a man of great love, especially for his family and close friends in the Dominicans, such as his assistant Reginald and his mentor Albert. He was generous to all, always responding to the needs and requests of others. His affective side, his tears and ecstasy, show that he was not a cold intellectual. Rather, Thomas was a person who gave his life to God and humanity. He was a priest who understood the human condition and recognized the merciful Christ, claiming that "the greater the sin the more it was the purpose of Christ's coming to wipe it out" (Aquinas, *Summa* III, 1, 4).

His dynamic preaching suggests that he could move easily between the theoretical and practical worlds. He was a man of powerful conviction and emotion—staying the course even in the face of opposition. He was also a man of creativity and imagination, and a risk taker. He forsook conventional wisdom by joining the Dominicans and then adroitly integrating the pagan philosopher Aristotle into his ideas and writings. Ironically, after his death, the bishops of Canterbury and Paris—moved by political concerns and theological ideologies—condemned some of his positions, casting a shadow on his work (those condemnations were not removed until a year after his canonization). Yet, paradoxically, this courageous man suffered from a phobia of lightning and storms, perhaps caused by a storm in his boyhood that killed his infant sister.

Pope John Paul II rightly proclaimed Thomas to be a model theologian. He was also much more than that. As preacher, teacher, friar, and man of prayer, Thomas offers us a model of Christian living, of the spiritual life and love.

The Spirituality of Thomas

To pray with Thomas Aquinas requires some understanding of his spirituality. All of Thomas's theological work, and his way of life, exemplify his profound spirituality. This is demonstrated by an exchange that is said to have taken place during the debate over whether to canonize him. One official raised the objection that only three miracles attributed to Thomas occurred during his lifetime. Supposedly, Pope John XXII countered by asserting that Thomas's theological work itself stood as miraculous. Recalling that the *Summa* was written in the format of questions and answers, the pope said that Thomas "worked as many miracles [in his lifetime] as questions he had determined" (Weisheipl, p. 347). These words capture the profound interconnectedness of theology, spirituality, and sanctity in the life and work of Thomas. (The argument of the pope prevailed, and Thomas was canonized in 1323.)

Thomas wrote nearly one hundred beautifully reasoned and spiritually profound works. The following summary only briefly describes some of the major themes of his spirituality:

The Beauty of Creation and the Human Person

Aquinas saw the world, the creation of God, as being good. He reasoned that our spiritual life does not involve escape from our bodily reality, nor does it imply that the world is evil or that one must enter a monastery in order to become holy. For Thomas, the goodness of God was clearly manifested through the diversity of creation. All of creation, and all that we do, contributes to our spirituality. Our bodies, our passions, our emotions, and our feelings are all part of the life of the Spirit. Although these elements can sometimes mislead us, to do without them would make us less human. It is no wonder that Thomas insisted that sins of passion are among the less serious sins. He was a man of tears, a man who wrote frequently of matters of the heart. Thomas would have seen it as a terrible mistake to eliminate our intuitions, feelings, and experience from our understanding of the spiritual journey, in favor of a coldly rational approach to our relationship with God.

Moreover, his sense of the beauty of creation (and of the human person in particular) led him away from the typical painful mortifications of ascetic life in the Middle Ages. Thomas's sense of austerity focused instead on intellectual discipline.

Thomas's recognition of the goodness of creation should be a welcome insight for people concerned with environmental issues. Although he maintained that one worships the God of creation, not the creation of God, his understanding of the beauty, complexity, and greatness of created reality moves us toward God. A contemporary Dominican scholar states Thomas's position this way: "The real mystery of things is not *what* they are, but *that* they are, and it is their sheer existence which leads us to talk about God. . . . The fact that things exist and act in their own right is the most telling indication that God is existing and acting in them" (Tugwell, pp. 212–213).

God as Our Call, Our Happiness

Thomas believed that just as the great variety within the created world manifests a complex and providential expression of God's goodness, so does the existence of each human being. God directs each created reality toward its own perfection; that implies that each human being has a unique role in building the Reign of God.

Thus, each of us has a vocation, a calling. Each of us takes a different path toward God. Thomas said that while we are made in the image and likeness of God, we are also made to move instinctually back to God. In moving back to God, each of us will have our own particular spirituality, with spiritual practices adapted to our own temperament. But all of us, with all our different pathways, seek happiness. And ultimate happiness lies in God alone. For Thomas, our natural happiness and enjoyment of the things of creation are quite appropriate as long as we keep our eyes fixed on our relationship with God.

Charity as Friendship with God

In Thomas's view, our relationship with God is best expressed by the notion of friendship. Love or charity is a type of friendship with God. Even today, when we think of analogies to express our relationship with God, what images come to mind? God as judge? God as invisible and incomprehensible being? God as ruler of the universe? God as parent? Thomas did not deny the truth of these analogies, but said that the best way of understanding God is as our *friend*, for that is what charity is.

But how can we be friends with God? How can the finite befriend the infinite? How can we form a friendship with a God we cannot see? Thomas was aware of these questions; he was aware, too, that Jesus told his disciples, "I do not call you servants any longer, . . . but I have called you friends" (John 15:15). For Thomas, Jesus represented the perfect bridge between the finite and infinite. Moreover, Thomas saw friendship as possible only because of the grace of God. Through Jesus, and by the power of the Holy Spirit, we become friends with the Father.

Several characteristics of human friendships carry over, by analogy, to charity, to friendship with God. One is that a true friendship is based on a willingness to spend time with the friend. Thus, we not only need to know *about* God, we also need to *know* God. The need to know God inspired Thomas to be a voracious reader of many different sources, testing them and integrating them into his spirituality insofar as they revealed the truth. For us, the desire to know God implies an openness to the truths of science, of non-Christian religions, and most especially of the Scriptures and the teachings of Christianity. For Aquinas, the need to know God in order to fashion a deepening friendship also pointed to the importance of prayer (which is discussed later in this introduction).

Another aspect of human friendship is that a friend desires the best for the other person. Aquinas believed that God indeed wants the best for us. Consequently, in his spirituality, Thomas placed a heavy emphasis on petitionary prayer, on asking God for the things we need in order to grow in Christian holiness. Today, some see petitionary prayer as self-serving, a lower form of prayer. Yet, Thomas envisioned it as the essence of prayer precisely because charity is a type of friendship with God wherein God wants what is best for us.

Finally, true friends start to emulate one another's good or virtuous qualities. As we grow in charity, Thomas said, we begin a process of transformation into the holiness of God. We become more attuned to the goodness of God and sensitized and repulsed by the evil of sin.

The Unity of Spirituality and Morality

Thomas's view of the connection between the moral life and spirituality was directly related to his view of our relationship with God as a transformative friendship. In the past few centuries, Christians have labored under an impoverished view of the moral life because the moral life has been severed from spirituality. We have struggled under the fear of punishment if a law is transgressed. We have adopted a simplistic approach to the moral life. This approach would have been entirely foreign to Aquinas precisely because he understood that our friendship with God evokes a kind of virtuous transformation prompted by the Holy Spirit.

Spirituality at its heart involves a growth in charity. Growth in charity necessarily entails an emphasis on all the other virtues because, according to Thomas, charity directs all other virtues toward their proper end, namely, God. For Aquinas, spiritual life may start with avoidance of sin, but it primarily involves growing in virtue. If we are formed in the virtues, then our actions generally will be good. Thus, part of our life of prayer is examining how we are progressing in the virtues.

Aquinas acknowledged that we do not become virtuous immediately. The moral virtues are by nature interior dispositions toward the good, and usually take time to acquire. Eventually, virtue becomes its own reward and source of joy. For Aquinas, and other Dominicans like Catherine of Siena a century later, we initially love God out of fear. Later, love of God is motivated in part by the promise of reward and the desire to be virtuous. Finally, we love God simply because of God's goodness. Thomas's approach to the acquisition of virtue is developmental in nature, and therefore allows for mistakes. In fact, Thomas recognized that at the beginning, the struggle between vice and virtue is strong, and we should not be discouraged by sin.

Building on the Virtues: The Life of Grace

If Aquinas was not discouraged by sin, it is because he was the pre-eminent theologian of the grace of God; that is, he proposed that the transformative process of becoming virtuous is rooted more in the grace of God than in our natural abilities. Thomas believed that grace—especially in the form of the gifts of the Holy Spirit—builds on our nature. Those infused gifts of the Spirit help us live out the virtuous life, thereby empowering us to grow in friendship with God. By analogy, the gifts of the Spirit allow us to walk smoothly toward a goal rather than stumbling or staggering toward it.

For Thomas, growth in the life of grace, toward the Father, in the Spirit, is grounded in Jesus. Thus, Thomas's spirituality is remarkably Trinitarian, weaving Father, Son, and Holy Spirit together in the graced life. Jesus is the supreme model of virtue; by grace, we are more and more conformed to him. Moreover, through the sacraments, the presence of Jesus is made real and helps us grow in the life of grace. Thomas had particular fondness and devotion for the Eucharist in his spirituality. He celebrated Mass daily and also assisted at another Mass. He often prayed in the presence of the Blessed Sacrament. Sometimes, he was caught up in such concentration and love while celebrating Mass that his server had to prod him to finish. And he composed texts on the Eucharist that are some of the most beautiful, affective, and profoundly theological in the history of the church. Aquinas firmly held that Jesus Christ is the way back to the Father.

A Spirituality of Preaching

Any introduction to the spirituality of Aquinas would be incomplete if it did not address that spirituality in the context of his Dominican vocation. Thomas was first and foremost a preacher in the tradition of Dominic. As such, he lived out the order's motto—To contemplate and to share with others the fruits of our contemplation. This contemplation was deeply rooted in the Scriptures, which Thomas believed needed to be encountered with five attitudes: listening, believing, meditating, communicating, and finally completing or actualizing in daily living (see Torrell, p. 32). His great *Summa* was in essence a commentary on the Scriptures. As a Dominican, then, Thomas practiced a spirituality of emulating Jesus, who was himself an itinerant preacher of the Gospel.

This brief excursion through the spirituality of Thomas shows that that spirituality is all-encompassing. It touches on traditional components like prayer and contemplation. Significantly, it also integrates his systematic work on morality, Christology, the sacraments, the Trinity, the understanding of the human person, and the Scriptures. That integration itself allowed Thomas to contemplate or gaze on God. It allows us to do the same.

Thomas on the Life of Prayer

Prayer is a major area of focus in Thomas's spirituality. Thomas asked important theoretical questions about prayer and addressed practical ones as well: What is prayer? How should we pray? What are the kinds of prayer? Why should we pray? To whom should we pray? What should we ask for in prayer? Should we ask God for particular things? Should we ask for temporal things? Is attentiveness necessary? Is prayer effective? Ought prayer to go on for a long time? Do sinners obtain anything from God by praying?

For Thomas, the answers to these questions were based on an understanding of prayer as an orderly attempt to ascertain and choose what is good by attuning our will to that of God. Petitionary prayer becomes the essence of that process. Thomas surmised that prayer is important because God is always close to us, wanting to help us (even if we do not feel that God is there). Because God is near to us, prayer is not complicated or mysterious or a skill requiring techniques that only the spiritually elite can master. Prayer is for everyone.

Some might believe that petitionary prayer is not useful, because God is already close to us and knows what we need and God's will is unchangeable. However, Aquinas argued that by God's design, we do cause things to occur when we petition God in prayer, not because we change God's will, but because God has willed that if we pray, certain things will happen. If we do not pray, those things will not happen. In asking for those things, we grow in recognizing our dependence on God and on the meaning of God's will for us.

When it came to prayer, Thomas was sympathetic. He understood well the limitations of the human condition. He recognized the distractions that can afflict us in prayer. He indicated that attentiveness is good, but the key to prayer is the initial intention we take into it. He noted that we need not pray to the point of weariness. He also explained that even when we are in serious sin, we can still be heard by God.

Thomas's position was practical. For instance, he espoused praying out loud even when alone because it may accomplish these things:

+ stir our devotion
+ keep our attention from wandering
+ increase the intensity of prayer, which leads to tears and jubilation
+ enable us to pray with our whole body

He taught that we should be specific in what we pray for, in order to focus our prayer, make ourselves more aware of what we need and desire, and entreat God more fervently.

In praying, Thomas recommended these steps:

1. Remember God's work in our life so as to strengthen our faith in petitionary prayer.
2. Make the petition.
3. Conclude with an act of thanksgiving.

For Thomas, this movement paralleled what we do in the Eucharist—we remember God's work in salvation history through the readings from the Scriptures, we plead for Christ's presence in the consecrated bread and wine, and finally we offer a prayer of thanksgiving.

Thomas for Today

The meditations that follow share some of the works, themes, and stories in the life of the great saint who was so optimistic about the human journey back to God. The ordering of the meditations reflects the pattern of Thomas's *Summa Theologiae* and its theme of coming from and returning to God, along with the Dominican theme of contemplating and of sharing with others the fruits of our contemplation.

Specifically, as Christians, we begin with God, especially as Trinity (meditation 1). From God and God's love flow the created order, which is good (meditation 2). In particular, as human beings, we are good and loved by God as the pinnacle of creation (meditation 3). Also as such, we are called to strive for true happiness (meditation 4). We seek this happiness through our own particular vocation (meditation 5). In living out our vocation, we grow especially in charity, which is a type of friendship with God (meditation 6). To help ourselves grow in love or charity, we rely on an overall growth in the life of virtue (meditation 7). However, grace builds on nature, and the virtues are elevated through the gifts of the Holy Spirit (meditation 8). This elevation of grace is most profoundly experienced in the Eucharist (meditation 9). Growth in the life of virtue and grace necessarily prompts us to pray for the things we need in order to continue to grow in love of God, neighbor, and self (meditation 10). In particular, a most fitting type of petitionary prayer is the Our Father, or Lord's Prayer (meditation 11). Through a life of prayer, we come to know and contemplate the divine; that is, we come to know the truth (meditation 12). This growth in wisdom is aided and strengthened by our study (meditation 13). We share the fruits of our prayer and study through our preaching, both formally and informally (meditation 14). Finally, we discover the sum of everything our life is ultimately about: "Nothing but you, O Lord" (meditation 15).

Through these meditations, may you grow in friendship with God until one day you can say, like Thomas did in his final hours, "I receive you, price of my soul's redemption, I receive you, . . . for love of whom I have studied, watched, labored" (Torrell, p. 293).

✧ **Meditation 1** ✧

The Trinity

Theme: Thomas often approached God through the mystery of the Trinity. He believed that through grace, people are invited into the mystery. The same mystery inspires Christians today to grow in intimacy with the living God.

Opening prayer: "Live, my Triune God, so live in me that all I do be done by Thee, that all I think and all I say be thy thoughts and words this day. Amen" (traditional aspiration, source unknown).

About Thomas

Because the mendicant religious orders were nontraditional and still quite new when Thomas entered the Dominicans, it is understandable that people debated their value. It is also understandable that Thomas was cajoled into entering the discussion. His feelings on the matter eventually found their way into his *Summa Theologiae*. There, Thomas identified three basic types of religious life: the strictly contemplative (such as that of the Cistercians), the active (such as that of the Hospitallers), and the mixed active-contemplative (such as that of the Dominicans). For adherents to the mixed traditions, life in the priory was contemplative and monastic, but outside the religious house, active ministry was normative.

It is also not surprising that Thomas concluded that the active-contemplative life, rooted in prayer and study and combined with a commitment to preaching and teaching, was the most excellent. To describe this dual-purposed life, he created a phrase that has become the motto of the Dominican order: *Contemplare et contemplata aliis tradere* (To contemplate and to share with others the fruits of our contemplation).

Thomas's opinion about the most excellent form of religious life was consistent with his understanding of the Trinity. He described the mystery of the Trinity as a community of the Three Divine Persons. That community has an inner life that is intimate and mutually relational. It is also the Godhead with a mission, a way of functioning actively within creation. Because the goal of created life is intimacy with the Divine, the most excellent way for a human person to grow in that intimacy is to pattern himself or herself on the trinitarian life. Accordingly, Thomas's understanding of the Trinity led him to teach that human life at its best cultivates friendship with God through prayer, and witnesses to that friendship by a gospel way of activity.

Pause: Who is the Blessed Trinity for you?

Thomas's Words

God destines us for an end beyond the grasp of reason. . . . Hence the necessity for our welfare that divine truths surpassing reason should be signified to us through divine revelation. (Aquinas, *Summa* I, 1, 1)

That person, therefore, who considers maturely and without qualification the first and final cause of the entire universe, namely God, is to be called supremely wise. . . .

Now holy teaching goes to God most personally as deepest origin and highest end, and that not only because of what can be gathered about him from creatures . . . but also because of what he alone knows about himself and yet discloses for others to share. Consequently holy teaching is called wisdom in the highest degree. (Aquinas, *Summa* I, 1, 6)

By natural reason we can know of God only what characterizes him necessarily as the source of all beings. . . . Now the creative power of God is shared by the whole Trinity; hence it goes with the unity of nature, not with the distinction of persons. Therefore through natural reason we can know what has to do with the unity of nature, but not with the distinction of persons [of the Trinity]. (Aquinas, *Summa* I, 32, 1)

[Augustine said,] *The Father is principle of the whole godhead.*

. . . The word "principle" means simply that from which . . . another comes forth. . . . Since, then, the Father is one from whom another originates, it follows that the Father is principle. (Aquinas, *Summa* I, 33, 1)

There are in God two only who proceed, namely the Son and the Holy Ghost. . . .

. . . We cannot conceive divine processions except as corresponding to actions which remain within the agent. Now in a spiritual and divine nature there are only two such actions, namely to understand and to will. Thus we are left with the only possible conclusion that in God there can be no procession other than that of the Word and that of Love. . . .

. . . God understands everything by one simple act, and in this way, too, he loves all things. . . . in him there is but one perfect Word and one perfect Love. And this manifests his abounding fruitfulness. (Aquinas, *Summa* I, 27, 5)

Reflection

It is not possible to comprehend fully the trinitarian God. In fact, Thomas explained, the best way we can describe God is by analogy. That is, our best description of God is simply the least incorrect description we can construct. God's magnificence is almost beyond human understanding, but not completely so.

One way theologians facilitate human understanding about God is to ponder the mystery of the Trinity, and two different approaches have made the Trinity easier to image. One approach centers around the internal, community life that the three persons of the Trinity share with one another. This is called the Immanent Trinity. The second approach considers the ways the members of the Trinity function in creation. This is known as the Economic Trinity.

In the Economic Trinity, each of the three persons can be primarily identified with an activity in the created order, even though all three persons are involved in all activity. Accordingly, the first person of the Trinity, the Father, is addressed as the Creator; the second person, Christ, is called the Redeemer; and the third person, the Holy Spirit, is known as the Sanctifier. The persons of the Trinity can be better understood through the use of these activity-related titles. When we increase our understanding of the persons of the Trinity, we can better emulate them and grow in God-likeness. Such thinking corresponds perfectly to Thomas's way of thinking, which is that intimacy with God is achieved by better understanding God.

✧ God the Creator brought everything that exists into being out of nothing. Human beings, created in God's image, participate in the life of the Creator by using their creative powers to benefit others. Such participation occurs, for example, when a loving couple brings a new child into the world, when a dancer takes the stage, when a homemaker makes a meal, and when a teacher prepares a lesson plan. Reflect on the ways that using your own creative powers has enlisted you as a partner with God the Creator. Strategize ways that you can be in partnership with God the Creator. Make a prayer of thanksgiving for the ability to share in God's life in this manner.

✧ God the Redeemer was born into a world that knew far too much about brokenness, pain, and alienation, and taught lessons of healing, peace, and reconciliation. In a gesture of intimacy, Christ invites us to share in his healing ministry and to continue it. We are partners with God the Redeemer when we support efforts to promote the reign of peace and justice, when we wipe away another's tear, when we bandage a scraped knee, when we struggle to sow reconciliation where discord has flourished. How do you act as a partner to the Redeemer? How are you an agent for peace, justice, and human dignity? Reflect on these questions and ask for Christ's guidance in pursuing the goals they imply.

✦ God the Sanctifier makes all things holy. We are drawn to the Spirit, who invites us to collaborate in the work of sanctification. We participate in the Spirit's mission by naming grace where we find it, by encouraging talent as it begins to manifest itself in young people, by affirming goodness in others, by championing that which is right, and so on. Contemplate the ways that you promote the presence of goodness in the world. How do you encourage wholesomeness, wholeness, and holiness in others? Assess those ways, make thanks for them, and beseech God to increase them in your life.

✦ The Divine Trinity models perfect community life for us. In the spirit of the Trinity, identify the people who make up your own primary community, whether it be a family group, a religious community, or a closely bonded circle of friends. Bring to mind the ways that your community supports you, nurtures you, challenges you, and helps you to be your best self. Give thanks for these people and for their roles in your life, and ask God to help you support others in their pursuit of the good.

✦ Use the Doxology (see the closing prayer of this meditation) as a mantra. Pray it thoughtfully and repeatedly.

✦ Place yourself in a prayerful, relaxed posture. Bring to mind the three persons of the Trinity. (You may find it helpful to use an image of the Trinity, such as an icon.) Imagine that the persons of the Trinity are about to enjoy a conversation with one another, and you are to be the topic! Then listen attentively to what each person has to say about you, and hear how the other two persons respond. What do you learn about yourself from this conversation? What do you learn about each person of the Trinity from this conversation? How does this conversation affect you?

✧ Create a litany addressing either the Triune God or the individual members of the Trinity. After each name, pray the words, *"Kyrie eleison"* ("Lord, have mercy"). Begin with the several names for God provided below, then add your own titles as they emerge in your prayer.

Holy Trinity, One God; *Kyrie eleison.*
Blessed and Undivided Unity; *Kyrie eleison.*
God, creator of the world; *Kyrie eleison.*
Abba; *Kyrie eleison.*
Jesus Christ, redeemer of the world; *Kyrie eleison.*
Christ Jesus, word of the Father; *Kyrie eleison.*
Holy Spirit, comforter of a struggling creation; *Kyrie eleison.*
God, the Holy Spirit; *Kyrie eleison.*
Divine Wisdom; *Kyrie eleison.*

Conclude the litany with the Doxology.

God's Word

And Jesus came and said to them, "All authority in heaven and on earth has been given to me. Go therefore and make disciples of all nations, baptizing them in the name of the Father and of the Son and of the Holy Spirit, and teaching them to obey everything that I have commanded you. And remember, I am with you always, to the end of the age." (Matthew 28:18–20)

Closing prayer:

Glory to the Father, and to the Son, and to the Holy Spirit: as it was in the beginning, is now, and will be forever.
Amen.
(Doxology, in ICEL, *Christian Prayer*, p. 689)

The Goodness of Creation

Theme: The created world, including human creation, is good. Emotions, will, intelligence, passions, and bodily existence are all important to one's prayer and spirituality.

Opening prayer: Creator God, every part of my being is a reflection of you. I want to be obedient to the command to "be," which you gave me the moment my life began, and I also desire to achieve the fullness for which you designed me. That fullness consists in being faithful to the call to goodness that you issued to everything that exists, at the moment of its creation. Help me to search more ardently for the path that leads to my full human potential.

About Thomas

Thomas's reputation as an intellectual is so strong that it may be difficult to imagine him anyplace but at his worktable, quill pen in hand, or in a classroom, teaching young scholars. We are not likely to picture Thomas on a walk in the woods enjoying the splendors of creation. His writings make it clear, however, that he was on intimate terms with creation and understood its theological meaning. One biographer points out that Thomas was physically vigorous and spent a great deal of time, both by choice and by necessity, outdoors:

Thomas . . . must have been a man of unusual energy, generosity (he composed twenty-six works at the request of others), and courage. Some have estimated that on his trips across Europe he walked over 9,000 miles. Fatiguing travels did not discourage him, for they enabled his educational enterprises and research. . . . People who knew him described him as approachable, patient, and kind. His writings present the same image of their author. (O'Meara, p. 34)

Pause: God created you and found you very good. What does that mean?

Thomas's Words

Distinctiveness and plurality of things is because the first agent, who is God, intended them. For he brought things into existence so that his goodness might be communicated to creatures and re-enacted through them. And because one single creature was not enough, he produced many and diverse, so that what was wanting in one expression of the divine goodness might be supplied by another, for goodness, which in God is single and all together, in creatures is multiple and scattered. Hence the whole universe less incompletely than one alone shares and represents his goodness. (Aquinas, *Summa* I, 47, 1)

Reflection

Thomas's major work was the ministry of study and teaching, a principal preoccupation of the Dominican order throughout its history. Study, especially of the sacred sciences, is so highly regarded in the Dominican order that its members are excused from community exercises (even liturgical prayer) if those exercises would disrupt it. This was even true when successful community life was gauged primarily by the presence of a well-disciplined and highly structured monastic routine.

Finding himself rooted in this highly important intellectual ministry, Thomas revealed a balance in his values and an appreciation for the activity of God, through his engagement in other pursuits that took him well beyond the theologian's desk. On the political level, he was willing to aid reigning monarchs. Perhaps more immediate to his own situation, he entered forcefully into the frequent debates regarding the rights of members of religious orders on the teaching faculties of the universities of his time.

On the relational level, he was known to be a loyal friend and a loving member of his family. He participated in casual moments of travel, meals, and social events in order to enjoy the company of others, yet quite often, he discovered a deeper understanding of God's truth in the midst of these activities. Some of the more notable stories of Thomas's informal instructions occur during these occasions. No dynamic in Thomas's life, no matter how frivolous, created a barrier between him and his reflection on the things of God.

The attentive companion of Thomas Aquinas will discover countless opportunities to meet God through the course of an ordinary day filled with life's routine events.

✧ Reflect on a recent everyday activity that you found enjoyable. Perhaps it was lunch with a friend, a dramatic or musical performance, a trip, or an interruption of the day's work to accomplish an errand. Recall the entire situation—what occurred, whom you encountered, what you accomplished, and so forth. Recognize the ordinariness of this scenario. Next, listen to God's account of the value, the blessedness, and the goodness that entered your life because of your participation in this event. How was this activity sacred in God's eyes? How are all your everyday events sacred in the eyes of God?

✧ Every law of nature is a gift from God. God's typical way of acting in our lives is experienced not so much in miraculous and extraordinary interventions as in the natural unfolding of the dynamics of life and relationships. Even if typical Christians today might be inclined to dismiss occasional reports of divine interventions, like miraculous healings, they will likely recognize God's presence in the natural processes God has created. God's miraculous activity can be observed in the healings that result from medical treatment, or the reconciliation that occurs through sincere conversation, or the counsel given to someone in need, or the recognition of personal limitations.

Focus on God's activity in nature and assess your life, your relationships, your activities, and your world today. Look for the presence of God's miraculous power. Where is God? How is God acting today? What special gifts is God sending your way? Examine your life as the arena for God's miraculous intervention. Claim God's gifts for what they are.

❖ Consider this short Scripture verse: "God saw everything that he had made, and indeed, it was very good" (Genesis 1:31). Now take note of the created realities you find it difficult to appreciate. Those might include people whom you find it difficult to like, necessary human dynamics that you find repulsive, and learning processes that require more patience than you have. Remind yourself that all of those are the work of God's hands. Read the Scripture verse again. Search for the goodness that is inherent in each of those challenging realities. Where is God in them? What does God want to do in your life through them?

❖ Thomas could see traces of God's perfection in God's creatures: strength in the rhinoceros, power in the ocean, beauty in a child's face, loveliness in the song of a bird. He was aware that God directed them each to their goal through the instincts God implanted in them and, in the case of humans, the capacities and talents God gave to them. Thomas recognized God's ongoing act of creation sustaining each of God's creatures in existence at every moment. Consider these questions: Who taught the seed to reach its roots into the moist soil, its stem and leaves toward the sunlight? Who taught newly hatched turtles to scamper to the ocean waters, the bird to build its nest, and the cat to purr? Recognize God's presence. Inhale the fragrance of a flower, feel the warmth of the sun on your skin. Gaze at the beauty of a spring landscape, a snow scene. Enjoy God's creation.

✧ Because Thomas affirmed the goodness of creation, he was less inclined toward some of the more rigorous physical penances and mortifications than were many of his contemporaries. Instead, when he perceived the need to grow in self-discipline, he tended to emphasize intellectual asceticism. This might mean he made a firm commitment to disciplined study, or to be more careful in avoiding distractions while he worked, or to be more constant at his work. Christian life demands the regular support of self-discipline to curb one's tendency toward sin while helping to develop loving and wholesome habits. Critique your spiritual life. Where is more self-discipline required? What positive forms of self-discipline can help you to achieve your goal? In the spirit of Thomas, who recognized the value of the things that delight us, create a strategy for developing some form of self-discipline that will encourage your growth in holiness. What can you do? How will you proceed?

✧ Care for creation is a significant responsibility of every Christian. Are you a passionate steward over the world's goods that have been entrusted to your care? Are you a friend of the environment? Make an examination of conscience over your own stewardship of creation. Resolving to be a better steward of creation is striving toward holiness. How strong is your resolve?

God's Word

Bless the Lord, all you works of the Lord.
Praise and exalt him above all forever.
Angels of the Lord, bless the Lord.
You heavens, bless the Lord.
All you waters above the heavens, bless the Lord.
All you hosts of the Lord, bless the Lord.
Sun and moon, bless the Lord.
Stars of heaven, bless the Lord.

Every shower and dew, bless the Lord.
All you winds, bless the Lord.
Fire and heat, bless the Lord.

Cold and chill, bless the Lord.
Dew and rain, bless the Lord.
Frost and chill, bless the Lord.
Ice and snow, bless the Lord.
Nights and days, bless the Lord.
Light and darkness, bless the Lord.
Lightnings and clouds, bless the Lord.

Let the earth bless the Lord.
Praise and exalt him above all forever.
Mountains and hills, bless the Lord.
Everything growing from the earth, bless the Lord.
You springs, bless the Lord.
Seas and rivers, bless the Lord.
You dolphins and all water creatures, bless the Lord.
All you birds of the air, bless the Lord.
All you beasts, wild and tame, bless the Lord.
[All you people], bless the Lord.

O Israel, bless the Lord.
Praise and exalt him above all forever.
Priests of the Lord, bless the Lord.
Servants of the Lord, bless the Lord.
Spirits and souls of the just, bless the Lord.
Holy men of humble heart, bless the Lord.
Hananiah, Azariah, Mishael, bless the Lord.
Praise and exalt him above all forever.

(Liturgical adaptation of Daniel 3:57–88, NAB,
from ICEL, *Christian Prayer,* pp. 708–709)

Closing prayer: Thomas named these the three greatest prayers: the Lord's Prayer, the Ave Maria, and the Apostles' Creed, which names God's creating, sanctifying, and redeeming role in all of creation. Ponder the creed reflectively:

I believe in God, the Father almighty,
    creator of heaven and earth.

I believe in Jesus Christ, his only Son, Our Lord.
    He was conceived by the power of the Holy Spirit
        and born of the Virgin Mary.

He suffered under Pontius Pilate,
    was crucified, died, and was buried.
He descended to the dead.
On the third day he rose again.
He ascended into heaven,
    and is seated at the right hand of the Father.
He will come again to judge the living and the dead.

I believe in the Holy Spirit,
    the holy catholic Church,
    the communion of saints,
    the forgiveness of sins,
    the resurrection of the body,
    and the life everlasting. Amen.

✦ Meditation 3 ✦

God's Unconditional Love

Theme: "God loves us not because we are good; we are good because God loves us." With these words, Aquinas demonstrates the reality of God's unconditional love for the human person and the person's ultimate reliance on God. Our true self-esteem derives from the intrinsic dignity that comes with being created by God's infinite love.

Opening prayer: O God, you are the source of all goodness. I believe that my true vocation is to respond to your call to holiness. Help me to achieve that holiness, by drawing me closer to yourself. The more I am with you, the closer I am to your infinite goodness, which is the source of all the good that is within me.

About Thomas

We often overlook God's love for us, which invests in us our true value. Many times, the inner gifts that mark a strong character are eclipsed by lesser, passing values. When Thomas Aquinas was a young friar, he was misunderstood and his true value went unrecognized. Apparently he was a large man, and perhaps he moved slowly. He was also rather deliberate and not quick to speak up. As a result of these traits, his peers developed the impression that he was poorly equipped intellectually. They made sport of him, unkindly, nicknaming him the Dumb Ox. On one occasion, a classmate took pity on him and offered to help Thomas with a difficult lesson they had been assigned. As the tutoring session unfolded, the volunteer found himself overwhelmed by the complexity of the material they were studying. At that point, the Dumb Ox quite humbly proceeded to explain the rest of the lesson to his would-be tutor. Thomas had understood the subject matter perfectly from the start.

By pondering this episode from Thomas's life, we are reminded that we risk missing much more than someone's talents when we judge them rashly and superficially; we risk missing their true goodness, which can be for all of us a bridge to greater holiness. A person's goodness is a real treasure, but a treasure that can be easily obscured by shortsightedness and thoughtless assumptions.

God delights when we find and claim God's gift of goodness in ourselves. When we have successfully striven for holiness, we have laid claim to God's choicest gift. Other attributes, such as those that measure earthly success, do not rate highly in God's hierarchy of values. Yet, often those are the attributes that people value most highly. Through Thomas's example, we are reminded to attend to the challenging task of focusing our sights on the one gift that is the most worthy of all: the holiness of God. We can grow in this gift by coming to know God better through prayer and adoration and by seeking out God's goodness in people and in other aspects of creation.

Pause: You are made in the image and likeness of God. What does that mean to you?

Thomas's Words

"He who loveth Me, will be loved by My Father" [John 14:21]. This at first sight seems absurd. For does God love us because we love Him? Far be it! Hence it is written in 1 John 4:10, "Not as though we had loved God, but because He hath first loved us." It must be remembered therefore, that anyone who loves Christ is not loved because he loves but because he was first loved by the Father. There-fore, we love the Son because the Father loves us. For true love has this quality, that it draws the love of the lover. "Yea I have loved thee with an everlasting love, therefore have I drawn thee, taken pity on thee" (Jeremiah 31:3). But the love of the Father is not separate from the love of the Son, for it is the same love for both Divine Persons. . . .

. . . God loves all things created. He loves them lim-itedly—even the very devils, because He wishes for every creature a certain good, namely, that they live and un-derstand and exist which are indeed good things. But on the other hand God loves those unlimitedly to whom He wishes every good, namely that they possess God Him-self; the possession of Whom is the possession of Truth, for God is Truth. . . .

. . . God . . . truly and unlimitedly manifests Him-self to those fortunate and blessed souls . . . through glory, which is the ultimate effect of future beatitude. (*Commentary on the Gospel of John, Chapter 14*, Aquinas, pp. 428–429)

Reflection

Thomas clearly chose to be intentional about spreading good-ness in his life, particularly through membership in the Do-minican order. His family was quite well off, and he could have chosen to retain the earthly goods that would have come his way. Even as the appropriateness of a church career was clari-fied quite early in his life, he faced options that would have ensured comfort and power. None of those options would necessarily have meant putting away the things of God or turning away from God's unconditional love; there was good in all of them. Yet, he made the difficult choice to pursue the option that would give him, with his particular personality and circumstances, the best opportunity for doing good. It is the passion for discovering God's goodness, claiming that gift, growing in it, and then encouraging others to seek it that made Thomas Aquinas a saint. Cultivating that same passion is the ingredient that will make saints of all of us.

✧ Do you believe that you are good because God loves you? Reflect on this question. Why is it important to come to terms with this issue?

✧ How well do you reverence people whom society has dismissed or condemned? Even when steeped in sin, every person has been created by God and possesses potential for good. God demands that we treat every individual with care. How well do you understand people whose dignity has been compromised in one way or another? What value for the world do you recognize in the street person, the death row inmate, the addict, the abortionist, the abuser, or whoever else you judge should be added to this list? What about those, especially, who have chosen their evil? Where do you see their value? Perhaps one of the most difficult challenges for a Christian is to see value in the one who seems to have violated some of our most fundamental communal values. Turn to God in this quandary. Ask God to help you to understand better the divine understanding. Listen to what God has to say on this issue.

✧ Do others see God's goodness reflected in you? Imagine that several of the people who love you the most are gathered for a conversation. Listen in on their conversation. What are they talking about? You! Allow the conversation to unfold, and follow it as this select group of people discusses one thing: your goodness.

✧ In your imagination, gather again the people who love you the most. This time, picture them discussing your growing edges. What about you do they wish you could strengthen, develop, or change? Hear them lovingly identify your weaknesses, your sins, and other areas in which you fall short of the pursuit of goodness. How will you respond to their concerns?

✧ Because Christian life is so unambiguous in its call to care first for others, Christians sometimes find themselves reticent to pray for themselves. If you sometimes find yourself in this position, let go of your reticence. Approach the God who loves you unconditionally and express your needs, your problems, your plans, and the desires of your heart. Simply tell God what you require and want.

✧ Take a walk or a drive. Recall that God, who is always with you, is your companion on this journey. With every thing that you encounter—whether it be a person, a building, an aspect of nature, or someplace that is special to you—bring to mind how it has helped others, has served them, or has benefited them. What you are bringing to mind is one of the ways that holiness unfolds in creation and surrounds you. Express your thanksgiving to God for this gift. Treasure its memory in your heart.

God's Word

We know that all things work together for good for those who love God, who are called according to his purpose. For those whom he foreknew he also predestined to be conformed to the image of his Son, in order that he might be the firstborn within a large family. And those whom he predestined he also called; and those whom he called he also justified; and those whom he justified he also glorified.

What then are we to say about these things? If God is for us, who is against us? He who did not withhold his own Son, but gave him up for all of us, will he not with him also give us everything else? Who will bring any charge against God's elect? It is God who justifies. Who is to condemn? It is Christ Jesus, who died, yes, who was raised, who is at the right hand of God, who indeed intercedes for us. (Romans 8:28–34)

Closing prayer: Touch me once again, O Holy One, with your transforming love. It is through my experience of your love that I am able to find my way to the holiness of life to which you beckon me.

✧ Meditation 4 ✧

Happiness

Theme: Human beings are made in the image and likeness of God, and seek happiness, both natural and supernatural. We come forth from God and are destined to return to God, the ultimate source of happiness.

Opening prayer: Loving God, source of all being, help me to grow in the conviction that true happiness, genuine holiness, and human wholesomeness are all one in the same: the attainment of the full human potential, which comes from ordering my life according to your divine image and likeness.

About Thomas

Thomas knew hardship, suffering, and pain. It seems that a younger sister met with a tragic death while Thomas was a small boy. Later, his family was so bitterly opposed to his Dominican vocation that they kidnapped him and imprisoned him for a time in an effort to dissuade him from joining the Friars Preachers. When he was about to become a theology professor, immense turmoil over the presence of the friars at the universities caused Thomas to feel the bitterness of some of his prospective colleagues. He had to participate in unkind debates on that issue, in his role as a major spokesperson for the friars. Later, he was frequently transferred from one city and country to another, at a time when travel was difficult and dangerous. Most of his assignments placed him at quite a distance from his beloved family.

Through these various episodes of suffering, and others, Thomas teaches an extraordinary lesson about happiness. The hardships he endured certainly hurt him, and he lived with their painful effects, but none of them could take away his happiness. Thomas knew that true happiness comes from being in right relationship with God. If our life is directed toward God, we have the inner happiness that enables us to sustain the gravest disappointments. This does not imply that the person in love with God does not experience suffering, or that love of God trivializes pains. In fact, the great sensitivity produced by friendship with God can actually heighten our sensitivity to pain. But the inevitable sadness, grief, and pain of human life do not have the power to obliterate the deeply rooted sense of happiness that comes from being in harmony with God.

Human life is imperfect, and so the happiness that comes from being in harmony with God in this life is incomplete. But it conveys a promise of the full and perfect happiness that will belong to the friends of God in the next life, when they will behold God for eternity in the Beatific Vision. Until then, Thomas's experience reveals that the happiness God brings into a relationship in the present, even though it lacks the completeness of eternity, is unassailable. Such happiness is extended to us all.

Pause: What is genuine happiness? What is its true source? Do you possess it?

Thomas's Words

We are told, Blessed are the clean of heart for they shall see God. . . .

. . . A right good will is required, both beforehand and during happiness.

The will is rightful when duly bent on its ultimate end, which end is to intermediate purposes as form to matter. Now as material cannot be shaped unless it be duly prepared, so likewise nothing gains its end unless it be well adapted to it. The inference is that nobody can come through to happiness without a right good will, which, therefore, is an antecedent condition.

It is also an attendant condition of final happiness, which . . . consists in the vision of the divine essence, which is goodness pure and unalloyed. And so the will of a person who sees God face to face must needs love whatsoever he loves within the embrace of God's goodness; to draw a parallel, even now the will of a person not seeing God must needs love whatsoever he does love within the common notion of goodness known to him. So is the will set straight, and final happiness cannot exist manifestly without this rightness. (Aquinas, *Summa* I-II, 4, 4)

Man's last and perfect beatitude, which he expects in the life to come, is wholly centred on contemplation. As for the imperfect beatitude we can have at present, it is primarily and chiefly centred on contemplation, secondarily on the activity of the practical intelligence governing our deeds and feelings. (Aquinas, *Summa* I-II, 3, 5)

Reflection

Thomas witnessed to the wholesomeness and the holiness that come from participating in delightful experiences. We know that he relished his life of study so much that at least once, he even forgot that he was at a festive meal with interesting company, and became deeply immersed in solving the problem he was working on at the time. Other stories relate that he sometimes so deeply enjoyed his intellectual and prayer pursuits that he levitated! Another describes, with humor, how he asked for some herring during his final illness. Why? Because he liked herring!

Thomas's life demonstrates that genuine happiness and the proper pursuit of legitimate pleasures are tools God has provided to assist us in our search for authenticity and holiness.

✧ Place yourself in a casual attitude of prayer, perhaps while taking a walk or listening to music. Call to mind the people, places, things, and events that bring you delight. What are your favorite things? Can you name them? Perhaps it would be helpful to write these them down. Simply ponder each of your favorite things as you call them to mind, and express your appreciation to God for each gift that brings you happiness.

✧ The Beatitudes (see "God's Word" later in this meditation) reveal that Jesus does not consider the attainment of comfort in this life to be the key to happiness. How do the values of Jesus find expression in your life? How are you poor in spirit, meek, hungry, thirsty, in mourning, persecuted, pure of heart, in pursuit of peace or mercy, insulted, or maligned? Once you have identified any of these realities as part of your life, reflect on how these difficult dynamics have indeed brought blessedness into your life. How has suffering helped you to grow holy? Be thankful for this strange kind of gift from God.

✧ What about you brings God happiness? Pray for help to become aware of what about you pleases God. Then ask God to show you the way to even deeper growth. How will you respond?

✧ In some scriptural translations, the Beatitudes begin with the words "Happy are they who." Use these words and write your own beatitudes: for example, "Happy are they who share, for theirs is the appreciation of those to whom they have been generous." Let the beatitudes flow from your heart. Write them down and pray them often, changing them as needed from time to time.

✧ You might also create beatitudes that use the names of people you love in the first part, and one of the reasons you love them in the second part. For example, "Blessed is my grandmother, for she has shown me an example of goodness." Make a prayer of thanksgiving for each of the people you name, as well as for the gift you identify.

✧ True happiness, as defined by the Gospels and explained by Thomas Aquinas, comes from God and is not identical to the state that many people define as happiness. Wealth, power, and prestige are just three of the false idols that people often identify as necessary for happiness. These and other passing goals that many associate with happiness are not in harmony with the deep happiness God intends for us all. Explore your own state of harmony with God. Enter into a dialogue with God, pray to Thomas Aquinas, and consult the wisdom figures in your life. In the presence of God, the source of all happiness, write your own definition of happiness.

God's Word

Blessed are the poor in spirit, for theirs is the kingdom of heaven.

Blessed are those who mourn, for they will be comforted.

Blessed are the meek, for they will inherit the earth.

Blessed are those who hunger and thirst for righteousness, for they will be filled.

Blessed are the merciful, for they will receive mercy.

Blessed are the pure in heart, for they will see God.

Blessed are the peacemakers, for they will be called children of God.

Blessed are those who are persecuted for righteousness' sake, for theirs is the kingdom of heaven.

Blessed are you when people revile you and persecute you and utter all kinds of evil against you falsely on my account. Rejoice and be glad, for your reward is great in heaven, for in the same way they persecuted the prophets who were before you. (Matthew 5:3–12)

Closing prayer: Loving God, you have created the smile, the twinkle in the happy eye, the gift of laughter, the delight of love, the fun of wholesome diversion, the warm feeling that comes from caring for others, the serenity that comes from inner peace, and the contentment of love. Help me to pursue the things that come from you. Help me to make the right choices so that I will value the things that will draw me into accord with your will, for it is in union with you through the pursuit of your will, that I will find my true happiness.

Our Response
to the Divine Call

Theme: Everyone has a role in establishing the Reign of God. Each person is created good, and God uses and builds on the talents of all through grace. This reality is described as grace building on nature. Through the diversity of human talents and gifts, the fullness of God's own goodness is manifested.

Opening prayer: O God, the source of my life, since the moment that you called me into being, you have drawn me to yourself. Help me to hear your voice, that I may always respond with trust and confidence. Let your word be the lamp that guides my feet.

About Thomas

There seems to have been little doubt among Thomas's family, even from his childhood, that he was destined to embrace a church career. However, the exact nature of Thomas's ecclesiastical career was another matter entirely. Thomas studied at the Benedictine abbey of Monte Cassino as a boy and probably became an oblate with the Benedictine order. As an oblate, he would have enjoyed a certain degree of formal association with the abbey, without taking vows or becoming a monk. It seems likely that the abbey and Thomas's family all presumed that eventually he would embrace the Benedictine life. Given his family's socioeconomic position, it was also probable that he would eventually become an abbot.

God's plan for Thomas, however, included neither membership in the great Benedictine order nor possession of an abbot's throne. During his adolescent studies at the University of Naples, Thomas was drawn to join the white-robed sons of Saint Dominic, known as the Friars Preachers. Thomas recognized his attraction to the Dominicans as a divine call, and he responded obediently by entering the novitiate. His family was outraged by Thomas's decision to join the begging friars, whose order was then too new to be able to guarantee stability or respectability. His family expressed its opposition by forcibly removing Thomas from the company of the friars and keeping him away from the order for more than a year.

Legends abound regarding this period of "captivity." Perhaps the most famous tale relates that a prostitute, probably hired by Thomas's brothers, was brought in to dissuade him from his vocation. The story goes that when the woman, whose dress and manner spelled seduction, entered Thomas's room, he responded with an emotional outburst and drove her out with a piece of burning wood from the fireplace. Thereafter, he remained fully convinced that he was to lead a life of chastity. Other stories maintain that Thomas was actually imprisoned in a cell throughout the time his family detained him, although the veracity of this claim is dubious.

What is clear from this episode is that neither the outrage of his family nor the promise of a brilliant career elsewhere could dissuade Thomas from responding to what he perceived to be the divine call in his life. By his obedient response to the divine call, he became a Dominican friar through whom God effected much good in the world.

Pause: Do you recognize your own life as an obedient response to God's many invitations?

Thomas's Words

It is the grace of the Holy Spirit, given through faith in Christ, which is predominant in the law of the New Covenant, and that in which its whole power consists. So before all else the New Law is the very grace of the Holy Spirit, given to those who believe in Christ. . . . Augustine says that *as the law of works was written on tablets of stone, so the law of faith is written in the hearts of the faithful.* And elsewhere in the same book he says, *What are the laws of God written by God himself in our hearts, if not the very presence of the Holy Spirit?*

There do however belong to the New Law certain elements which in a way dispose us for the grace of the Holy Spirit, and some which are concerned with its exercise. These may be considered secondary in the New Law, and Christ's faithful had to be instructed about them both orally and in writing, both as regards matters of faith and as regards actions. Hence the New Law is first and foremost an inward law, and secondarily a written law. . . .

. . . Something can be inward to man in two ways. Firstly, with reference to human nature; in this sense the natural law is inward to man. Secondly, something may be inward to man as though added on to nature by the gift of grace. It is in this sense that the New Law is inward to man; it not only points out to him what he should do, but assists him actually to do it.

. . . No one has ever had the grace of the Holy Spirit except by faith in Christ, whether this faith be explicit or implicit. Now by faith in Christ man belongs to the New Covenant. Hence anyone who received the law of grace inwardly by this very fact belonged to the New Covenant. (Aquinas, *Summa* I-II, 106, 1)

Reflection

The pursuit of the *voluntas Dei*, "the will of God," is a classical feature of the Christian vocation. Unfortunately, many people believe that cooperation with God's will necessarily involves consistently choosing the most challenging option available or the path most strewn with excessive asceticism. Through his support of the scholastic axiom that grace builds on nature, Thomas clarified that God's will is often fulfilled by acting on one's own wholesome inclinations.

Apart from any inclination toward sin, the Christian can typically trust that God's will is to be found in the desires of our own heart, in the pursuit of that which brings delight to self and to others. Naturally, the Christian will want to develop the habit of filtering desires and inclinations through the screen of gospel love, but with that habit in place, a sound Thomistic spirituality leads to the searching of the heart in order to hear the promptings of the Holy Spirit.

✧ What pressures or realities prevent you from following your call? What stands in the way of your becoming all that God has called you to be? What holds you back? What obstructs growth? Identify those barriers and seek God's help in constructing ways around them.

✧ Identify a decision you will face within the next several days. Reflect on what God's desire might be regarding this matter, recalling that no issue that affects you is insignificant to God. Does it seem that greater good can be accomplished by any of the options at your disposal? Does any particular plan of action seem to resonate more clearly with God's will? Proceed with your discernment in conversation with God. Listen for the divine call, and plan to respond accordingly.

✧ Take a personal inventory of the significant good decisions you have made throughout your life. How have your choices nurtured the presence of God's goodness in your life and in the lives of the people with whom you are involved? Make a prayer of thanksgiving for the privilege of participating in the spread of God's goodness through your various choices.

✧ Recall instances in which you have made the wrong choices. How has God been faithfully present to you even in those moments? How has the presence of the faithful God helped you to survive and even grow from your mistakes?

✧ Take an inventory of the treasures of your life. Whom do you love? What about your loved ones draws you to them? What are your greatest values? What are your passions? What energizes you? What are your hobbies? What do you collect? What are your favorite diversions? Ask yourself how those treasures parallel the values communicated through the Gospel of Jesus Christ. Are your treasures "of God"?

God's Word

"The word is near you,
on your lips and in your heart"
(that is, the word of faith that we proclaim); because if you confess with your lips that Jesus is Lord and believe in your heart that God raised him from the dead, you will

be saved. For one believes with the heart and so is justified, and one confesses with the mouth and so is saved.
The scripture says, "No one who believes in him will be
put to shame." For there is no distinction between Jew
and Greek; the same Lord is Lord of all and is generous to
all who call on him. For, "Everyone who calls on the
name of the Lord shall be saved." (Romans 10:8–13)

Closing prayer:

O merciful God, grant that I may
      desire ardently,
      search prudently,
      recognize truly,
      and bring to perfect completion
    whatever is pleasing to You
      for the praise and glory of Your name.
                (Aquinas, *Devoutly I Adore Thee,* p. 5)

Friendship with God

Theme: Charity, the pinnacle of Christian life, is imaged as a deep and abiding friendship with a loving God. When we reach this pinnacle, we are no longer servants; we are now friends, through the merit of Christ. As friends, we are called to spend time with God, not only to know *about* God but to *know* God personally through the grace of the Holy Spirit, and to grow in likeness to this friend.

Opening prayer: Divine Friend, you have extended the gift of your friendship to me. Your friendship is a priceless treasure; help me to understand better the nature of this gift as well as the responsibilities that accompany it. Friendship with you results in greater love of neighbor. Let the quality of my interactions with others always serve me as a signal of the quality of the relationship that you and I share. Move me always to greater love of you, my neighbor, and myself; in that love, I will always know that I am the faithful friend you want me to be.

About Thomas

Thomas's search for friendship with God was the bedrock of his entire life. He seems to have been one of those especially graced souls whose fascination with God was apparent from a tender age.

Thomas's formal education began at the Benedictine abbey school of Monte Cassino. One day, when Thomas was perhaps as young as five years old, he was participating in a catechism lesson. During the class, the monk who was teaching referred to God a number of times. After a while, Thomas called out a question that would characterize his entire life's pursuit: "But teacher, what *is* God?"

Thomas never stopped asking that question, and in cultivating his interest in God, he grew in friendship with the divine one. Aquinas teaches us that friendship with God, a relationship infused by the Holy Spirit, is an interpersonal process that requires nurture and fidelity.

Pause: How is your relationship with God typical of the relationship that exists between two friends?

Thomas's Words

The Lord's words, *No longer will I call you servants but my friends,* can be explained only in terms of charity, which, therefore, is friendship.

. . . Not all love has the character of friendship, but that only which goes with well wishing, namely when we so love another as to will what is good for him. For if what we will is our own good, as when we love wine or a horse or the like, it is a love not of friendship but of desire. . . .

Yet goodwill alone is not enough for friendship for this requires a mutual loving . . . based on something in common.

Now there is a sharing of man with God by his sharing his happiness with us, and it is on this that a friendship is based. . . . Now the love which is based on this sort of fellowship is charity. Accordingly it is clear that charity is a friendship of man and God. (Aquinas, *Summa* II-II, 23, 1)

Charity . . . is our friendship for God arising from our sharing in eternal happiness, which is not a matter of natural goods but of gifts of grace. . . . We have it neither by nature, nor as acquired, but as infused by the Holy Spirit, who is the love of the Father and the Son; our participation in this love . . . is creaturely charity itself. (Aquinas, *Summa* II-II, 24, 2)

Now the light in which we must love our neighbour is God, for what we ought to love in him is that he be in God. Hence it is clear that it is specifically the same act which loves God and loves neighbour. And on this account charity extends not merely to the love of God, but also to the love of neighbour. (Aquinas, *Summa* II-II, 25, 1)

Reflection

Parents express a great deal of concern over the company their children keep. Proper vigilance over the relationships of young people is an exacting parental responsibility, for as an old adage says, We tend to behave like the company we keep.

There are different kinds of friends. Some friends encourage us, and others entice us to be reckless; some friends comfort, and others inspire. Some friends are good, and unfortunately some are bad. The best kind of friend encourages goodness in the other. When, in a particular relationship, we have found someone who consistently encourages habits that reflect the values of the Gospels, we have found the best kind of friend. We have found a treasure. God is that kind of friend.

God, who offers us a share of eternal happiness, desires for us all to become more like God. Vatican Council II identified God's desire as the universal call to holiness. We grow in holiness through prayer—by spending intimate time visiting with God, we come to know God better. The more we know God, the more we are drawn in to being more *like* God. Because God is love, a friend of God who wishes to become more like God becomes more loving. Hence, those who love God love others, and their love for others is the sign that they are in love with God.

✧ Call to mind several close friends. One by one, identify the outstanding virtue or attribute of each friend. Ask yourself how you have grown in that virtue or attribute as a result of your association with that friend. Friends whose presence leads us to greater goodness are the best kind of friends because they reflect God's friendship with us. Make a prayer of gratitude for your friends, and resolve to continue to grow in the virtues they have shared with you.

✧ There are many valid images of God. Some invite intimacy, others reveal God's grandeur, and others emphasize God's role as judge or source of justice. The teachings of Jesus indicate that God wants us to be intimate and comfortable with God: "I have called you friends, because I have made known to you everything that I have heard from my Father" (John 15:15). Ask yourself these questions: Do you see God as a friend? Do you spend enough time with that friend? What prevents you from spending more time with God in prayer? Ponder the elements of your life that stand between you and a closer friendship with God. Once you have named the barriers, they can be more easily addressed. Be attentive to whatever you need in order to cultivate a more prayerful life with God as your friend. What do you require?

✧ Choose a symbol for God that you can carry with you throughout the day. When you are at work, place that symbol within your view. When you are at the table for a meal, place it on the table. When you rest, place it near your bed. When you are enjoying music or television, place the object somewhere near you. Throughout the day, whenever you note the presence of the symbol, acknowledge God's constant companionship and communicate briefly with your divine companion. If you find this exercise especially helpful and would like to develop a daily habit of this nature, use several different objects, perhaps one for each day of the week. Alternate their use to avoid becoming so accustomed to a particular object that you take it for granted.

✧ Thomas wrote that charity is a type of friendship with God. In other words, our love of neighbor demonstrates our friendship with God. How does your practice of charity demonstrate that you are a friend of God's? Examine your current way of living for evidence of charity. Does your examination reveal that your friendship with God is healthy? If so, determine to grow in this regard. If you judge yourself wanting in this self-examination, make a prayer of thanksgiving for God's mercy and reflect on the words of Jesus in John 15:12–15 (see "God's Word" below). How will you respond? What shall you become? How can you make room in your life for the virtue of charity to grow?

✧ It is probably impossible for someone to love others without first having a sense of self-love. Do you love yourself? Are you a friend to yourself? Do you like who you are? If you are going to spend an evening or a day or a weekend alone, will you be in good company? Spend this prayer time noting the ways you like yourself, the ways others appreciate you, and the ways this world is a better place because you are here. See yourself as God sees you. What is the beauty that God sees when beholding you? What is the goodness that gives God delight when beholding you? Allow yourself to enjoy this reflection, and pay no attention to the faults that are also part of your life but which you can address at another time. How does it feel to like yourself? How does liking yourself strengthen you? Make a litany prayer of thanksgiving in your own words for all that you are.

God's Word

This is my commandment, that you love one another as I have loved you. No one has greater love than this, to lay down one's life for one's friends. You are my friends if you do what I command you. I do not call you servants any longer, because the servant does not know what the master is doing; but I have called you friends, because I have made known to you everything that I have heard from my Father. (John 15:12–15)

Closing prayer:

O most gentle God, who, foreseeing our desire, have imprinted Your image in our soul, we pray You in the name of all that You are, and by all that You are, to deign also mercifully to imprint in us Your divine ways. We ask this in order that Your labor for us be not lost, and that our life be not in vain nor given over to peril, should we fail to employ for our true end the care that You have taken of us. (Aquinas, *The Ways of God*, p. 79)

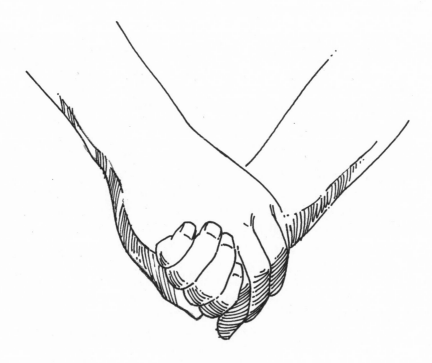

✧ **Meditation 7** ✧

Virtue

Theme: The moral life is tied to spirituality through the virtues. By growing in virtue, the human person grows in holiness. The Christian life, which is a process or journey, consists not in a minimalist avoidance of sin, but in growth in the habits of holiness.

Opening prayer: Loving God, source and goal of my life's journey, I turn over to you the direction of my life. At each stage, guide me closer to your own path. Let each day be for me an experience of growth in virtue so that as I age, my way will be nothing but a reflection of your own divine way.

About Thomas

Religious orders often feature a custom known as refectory reading, in which religious literature is read aloud by one member while the rest of the community eats in silence. This custom was in effect in Thomas's time. Being called to read could be a daunting challenge to the youngest and newest community members, for the community's superior (or another designated individual) had the responsibility to correct any mispronunciations or other mistakes the reader made.

Early in Thomas's religious life, his turn to be the reader came up, and he dutifully ascended the podium and began. At one point, the superior announced that Thomas had mispronounced a word. The superior corrected the pronunciation and indicated that Thomas was to repeat the word accordingly. Thomas accepted the correction, repeated the word as expected, and continued the reading. Later in the day, the superior realized that Thomas's pronunciation, and not his, had been correct. With that clarification, the community understood the depths of Thomas's humility.

Thomas's behavior in this instance demonstrates that virtue is nurtured by the development of habit. If we can graciously accept a correction, even an incorrect one, then we have traveled far on the road to humility.

Pause: What is your greatest virtue? What about you brings the ways of God closer to others' experience?

Thomas's Words

Augustine [wrote], *As soon as charity is born it is fed,* a reference to beginners; *fed, it grows strong,* a reference to those making progress; *grown strong it becomes perfect,* which applies to the perfect. Accordingly there are three degrees of charity. . . .

. . . Various stages can be marked according as growth in charity leads a man to fix his main attention on different things. For, to begin with, he must devote himself mainly to withdrawing from sin and resisting the appetites, which drive him in the opposite direction to charity. This is the condition of beginners, who need to nourish and carefully foster charity to prevent its being lost. A second stage now follows, when a man's chief preoccupation is to advance in virtue. This is the mark of those who are making progress, and who are principally concerned that their charity should grow and become strong. The third stage is when a man applies himself chiefly to the work of cleaving to God and enjoying him, which is characteristic of the perfect who *long to depart and to be with Christ* [Philippians 1:23]. (Aquinas, *Summa* II-II, 24, 9)

Reflection

Love does amazing things to people. For example, one hot Sunday afternoon, a carload of friends drove down an unfamiliar road. Their business was urgent. A record-breaking heat wave was in progress, and even with the air conditioner on at full blast, the car was uncomfortable. The friends agreed that nothing but the urgency of their own business could have taken them out of their comfortable homes on such a day.

Then, in the distance, they sighted a large crowd of people milling about a schoolyard. They could not imagine what event could entice people to be out in such weather. "No one in their right mind would choose to be out today," they exclaimed. What kind of people were these? As they came closer to the schoolyard, they understood immediately, for they saw a large sign that read: "Saint Clare School Band Parents' Flea Market. Help Send Our Kids to Band Camp." Of course, the friends realized, the kind of people who would be out on such an uncomfortable day were parents who saw an opportunity to benefit their children!

Good parents do not merely provide the basic essentials for their children; they also endeavor to afford every opportunity that they can, with little attention to the personal cost. The selfless love that parents shower on their children in a healthy family is an excellent symbol for the generous outpouring of self that God asks of those who desire holiness. The conscientious Christian does not merely avoid wrongdoing so as to avoid God's just punishment in the next life; the careful Christian cultivates the habit of magnanimity, of going the extra mile for others. The tendency to go that extra mile is not easily acquired; it is the product of a disciplined, hard-earned habit of living and caring for others. When such a good skill is acquired, it is a virtue, a good and consistent way of dealing with life's problems.

Thomas understood that virtue often develops gradually. Accordingly, the friend of God is committed to growing in holiness by cultivating virtuous habits in daily life. Vice stands in the way of growth in virtue, so it is essential to root out sin habitually. That is one reason that the Catholic church highly values the regular celebration of the sacrament of Reconciliation; reconciliation helps to identify and stifle the growth of sin, in an effort to nurture virtue.

✧ Examine your conscience. Identify the vices, or dispositions toward wrongdoing, that hinder your spiritual growth. Using your own words or the traditional Act of Contrition (the prayer recited by penitents participating in the sacrament of Reconciliation), express to God your sorrow for your sins and ask for forgiveness. Finally, ask for God's help in overcoming the sin in your life.

✧ In the spirituality of Thomas's day, Christian morality and Christian spirituality (the life of virtue) were regarded as one unified system of Christian study. Today, morality and spirituality are commonly approached as two different disciplines. Separating the two creates the risk of cultivating an improper emphasis on the mere avoidance of sin and evil, rather than cultivating an emphasis on magnanimous growth in the virtuous life. Morality becomes a mere mechanical following of rules to avoid wrongdoing, bereft of spiritual content, passion, and the desire to be perfect as God is perfect. Where do you stand on this issue? Is Christian life for you a mere avoidance of sin, or is it a daring challenge to the passionate pursuit of holiness? How might you adjust your approach to your Christian vocation?

✧ Take an inventory of your own virtues. What strains of the gospel message do you live habitually? Name your virtues. (In naming our virtues, we claim them as our own.) Try to recall how those virtues were planted in your life. Perhaps a parent, relative, or teacher helped you to achieve a certain virtue; perhaps a painful episode in life moved another to prominence for you. Ask God to help you grow even more deeply into this way of holiness. Listen for God's invitation. How does God want you to proceed?

✧ What virtue that you admire in others do you find insufficiently developed in your own life? Ask for God's help in developing that virtue; plan realistic ways to develop a habit of exercising that virtue. Place the fruit of your reflection in God's hands, and ask for divine assistance in achieving that goal.

✧ The three theological virtues are faith, hope, and charity. Make a drawing to serve as an icon or symbol for each of these virtues. Reflect and pray about each one. Address God by a corresponding title or name. Discuss with God your relation to each virtue (its meaning, its challenges, and its riches for you), and ask God for whatever insight or support you need in order to grow in that virtue.

✧ The cardinal virtues are prudence, justice, temperance, and fortitude. Many other virtues flow from these. Again, using an icon or symbol, pray over these, one at a time. Examine your own understanding of each virtue. What does its name mean? What does it describe? How does it challenge you? How does it describe a piece of your own life story? If you find it helpful, write out your definition of each virtue and answer these questions in writing.

God's Word

Therefore, since we are justified by faith, we have peace with God through our Lord Jesus Christ, through whom we have obtained access to this grace in which we stand; and we boast in our hope of sharing the glory of God. And not only that, but we also boast in our sufferings, knowing that suffering produces endurance, and endurance produces character, and character produces hope, and hope does not disappoint us, because God's love has been poured into our hearts through the Holy Spirit that has been given to us. (Romans 5:1–5)

Closing prayer:

O God,
    all-powerful and all-knowing,
    without beginning and without end,
You Who are
    the source,
    the sustainer,
    and the rewarder of all virtues,

Grant that I may
    abide on the firm ground of faith,
    be sheltered by an impregnable shield of hope,
    and be adorned in the bridal garment of charity.

Grant that I may
    through justice
        be subject to You,
    through prudence
        avoid the beguilements of the devil,
    through temperance
        exercise restraint,
    and through fortitude
        endure adversity with patience.

. . . .

Amen.

(Aquinas, *Devoutly I Adore Thee*, pp. 33–39)

✧ Meditation 8 ✧

The Gifts of the Holy Spirit

Theme: The Gifts of the Holy Spirit—wisdom, piety, counsel, fortitude, fear of God, understanding, and knowledge—help the Christian develop the virtuous life. Grace builds on nature, bringing forth the basic goodness inherent in all.

Opening prayer:

God of light, from whom every good gift comes, send your spirit into my life with the power of a mighty wind, and by the flame of your wisdom, open the horizons of my mind.

Loosen my tongue to sing your praise in words beyond the power of speech, for without your spirit, I could never raise my voice in words of peace or announce the truth that Jesus is Lord, who lives and reigns with you and the Holy Spirit, one God, for ever and ever. (Adapted from the alternative opening prayer for Mass on Pentecost)

About Thomas

Thomas knew that the success of all his projects depended on the activity and gifts of the Holy Spirit in his life. When faced with a significant project or a daunting problem, Thomas invoked the guidance of the Holy Spirit. In fact, Thomas appealed to the Holy Spirit to bless and guide every one of his activities, no matter how mundane.

When approaching his study table to write, prepare a lesson, plan a sermon, or dictate a theological text to a secretary, Thomas always asked the Holy Spirit for the gift of wisdom. One of the most learned men in Christian history, he delivered a profound lesson on the importance of placing one's confidence in God, by never beginning to teach without first entering into prayer, asking of God the gift of wisdom once again.

Thomas lived with a profound realization that the seven gifts of the Holy Spirit were always at his disposal, and his example continues to teach us the same.

Pause: When faced with a challenge, do you remember to ask, with confidence, for the support and direction of the Holy Spirit?

Thomas's Words

Taken as a personal name, "Gift" is proper to the Holy Spirit. To understand why, reflect that a gift, according to Aristotle, is literally a giving that can have no return, i.e. it is not given with repayment in mind and as such denotes a giving out of good will. Now the basis for such gracious giving is love; the reason we give something to another spontaneously is that we will good to him. And so what we give first to anyone is the love with which we love him. Clearly, then, love has the quality of being our first gift; through love we give all other loving gifts. Since, then, . . . the Holy Spirit comes forth as Love, he proceeds as being the first Gift. So Augustine teaches that *through the Gift who is the Holy Spirit, the many individual gifts are distributed to Christ's members.*

. . . In that the Son proceeds in the manner of a word, which in its meaning includes being the likeness of its source, he has "Image" as a proper name, even though the Holy Spirit is also like the Father. So too in that the Holy Spirit proceeds from the Father by way of love, he has "Gift" as a proper name, even though the Son is also given; and the very source of the Son's being given is the Father's love; *God so loved the world as to give his only begotten Son.* . . .

. . . Before being given a gift belongs to the giver alone; once given, however, it belongs to the recipient. . . . the divine Gift . . . is the Gift alone of God who gives. Once given, however, he then becomes the Spirit of someone or the One Given to someone. (Aquinas, *Summa* I, 38, 2)

Reflection

Ideally, gifts are given at the choice of the giver, out of a spirit of care or generosity. But the nature of a gift and the meaning of gift giving have become tremendously misunderstood in our culture. In some respects, gifts have come to be understood as the just payment for something that is due. Children are taught that it is their right to expect bundles of candy at Halloween; their expectation of significantly larger bundles at Christmastime is even more firmly established.

Such expectations continue into adulthood. Several years ago, a company promoted its product as the "perfect gift." In a television commercial, a man was surrounded by unacceptable gifts given by his mother on past Christmases. He held up the desired product for view, accompanied by the words: "This year, Mother, get it right! Buy this for me!" What is the operating definition of a gift here? We annihilate the integrity of gift giving when we forget that a gift is freely offered, cannot be demanded by the recipient, and cannot be given as payment for something that is due.

Consider, by way of contrast, a gift given by a young child to his or her mother—a gift of dandelions, perhaps, offered freely and joyously with no expectations. Or the gift of time and presence given by a hospice volunteer to a person dying of AIDS—again, offered freely, with no expectation of or desire for anything in return. It is hard to imagine either of these gifts being rejected by the recipient because the giver failed to "get it right."

The gifts of the Holy Spirit are likewise freely given. They manifest God's generosity and love for us, and they connect us, the recipients, to the Divine Giver. Receiving God's gifts causes us to become more like God: "Be perfect, therefore, as your heavenly Father is perfect" (Matthew 5:48). Finally, God's gifts to us become the perfect gifts—the gifts that we desire to share with others.

✦ Examine your life. What gifts—graces, virtues, abilities, talents, skills, positive dispositions, and so on—has God given you? Reflect on those gifts. Acknowledge them as coming from God. Then review the ways you share those gifts with others. How do you place the gifts God has given you at the service of humankind and creation?

✦ God knows precisely what we need to grow in holiness, and God's distribution of gifts corresponds to that understanding. The graced life that God grants us allows us to live the Christian life more easily. Bring to mind the seven gifts of the Holy Spirit. Reflectively define and come to terms with each of them: wisdom, piety, counsel, fortitude, fear of God, understanding, and knowledge. How has each of these gifts become part of your life? What good has each of these gifts empowered you to accomplish?

✦ Have you experienced a moment, or longer, of being aware that God's grace seemed to be especially at work in you? If so, what was going on at that time? What did this dynamic do to you? How did you respond? What does it mean to experience God's activity at work within you? Putting this experience (or experiences) into words or representing it somehow through art or movement can help you to claim it more deeply.

✦ Environment and ambience significantly influence people. Owners of restaurants, designers of hotels and public buildings, and teachers in classrooms all know the importance of creating the most conducive environment possible for achieving their purposes. In a similar way, arranging our physical and mental environments to help us recall that we are in

God's presence at all times moves us to grow in holiness. Does your environment, at home or work, facilitate your awareness of God's faithful and constant presence? You might try keeping a symbol of God (traditional or otherwise) visible throughout the day. On a more interior level, you might employ the simple devotion of jotting the letters *JMJ* (for Jesus, Mary, Joseph) at the top of a piece of paper on which you are about to write, or regarding every knock on the door as a recollection of Jesus' journey to Emmaus, and receiving each guest with the same hospitality you would offer to him. Study your environment. Does your space help draw your mind to God? Does it convey, at least in a subtle manner, Christian values? Is it hospitable to guests? Think about ways to make your environment more conducive to recognizing God's presence. Pray over it. Plan. Act.

God's Word

Now there are varieties of gifts, but the same Spirit; and there are varieties of services, but the same Lord; and there are varieties of activities, but it is the same God who activates all of them in everyone. To each is given the manifestation of the Spirit for the common good. To one is given through the Spirit the utterance of wisdom, and to another the utterance of knowledge according to the same Spirit, to another faith by the same Spirit, to another gifts of healing by the one Spirit, to another the working of miracles, to another prophecy, to another the discernment of spirits, to another various kinds of tongues, to another the interpretation of tongues. All these are activated by one and the same Spirit, who allots to each one individually just as the Spirit chooses. (1 Corinthians 12:4–11)

Closing prayer:

Come, Holy Spirit, come!
And from your celestial home
    Shed a ray of light divine!

Come, Father of the poor!
Come, source of all our store!
    Come, within our bosoms shine!

You, of comforters the best;
You, the soul's most welcome guest;
    Sweet refreshment here below;

In our labor, rest most sweet;
Grateful coolness in the heat;
    Solace in the midst of woe.

O most blessed Light divine,
Shine within these hearts of yours,
    And our inmost being fill!

Where you are not, man has naught,
Nothing good in deed or thought,
    Nothing free from taint of ill.

Heal our wounds, our strength renew;
On our dryness pour your dew;
   Wash the stains of guilt away:

Bend the stubborn heart and will;
Melt the frozen, warm the chill;
   Guide the steps that go astray.

On the faithful, who adore
And confess you, evermore
   In your sev'nfold gift descend;

Give them virtue's sure reward;
Give them your salvation, Lord;
   Give them joys that never end. Amen.
     Alleluia.

(The Sequence for Pentecost Sunday, in Catholic Book
Publishing Company, *Lectionary*, p. 135)

Corpus Christi

Theme: Aquinas had a tremendous devotion to the Mass and to the Blessed Sacrament. Love for the sacrament of Christ's body and blood remained at the heart of his spirituality, as a way of knowing Jesus Christ.

Opening prayer: "How holy this feast in which Christ is our food; his passion is recalled; grace fills our hearts; and we receive a pledge of the glory to come, alleluia" (ICEL, *Christian Prayer*, p. 661).

About Thomas

Thomas espoused a eucharistic spirituality that engendered profound intimacy with Christ. In Thomas's day, the church made significant strides in refining its appreciation and understanding of the eucharistic presence. In 1264, Pope Urban IV instituted the feast of Corpus Christi (which means, in Latin, "body of Christ"), and he commissioned Thomas to write the liturgical texts for the new feast. This was a labor love for Thomas, whose spiritual life was anchored in the Eucharist. As he expressed it in his eucharistic hymn entitled "O Salutaris Hostia," Thomas believed the Eucharist to be "the gate of heaven to all below."

Pause: One memorial acclamation the church uses at Mass announces,

When we eat this bread and drink this cup,
we proclaim your death, Lord Jesus,
until you come in glory.

How is your reception of the Eucharist a proclamation of the death of Jesus Christ, whose glorious return we await?

Thomas's Words

Since it was the will of God's only-begotten Son that men should share in his divinity, he assumed our nature in order that by becoming man he might make men gods. . . . He offered his body to God the Father on the altar of the cross as a sacrifice for our reconciliation. He shed his blood for our ransom and purification. . . . But to ensure that the memory of so great a gift would abide with us for ever, he left his body as food and his blood as drink for the faithful to consume in the form of bread and wine.

. . . Christ himself, the true God, is set before us as our food. What could be more wonderful than this? No other sacrament has greater healing power; through it sins are purged away, virtues are increased, and the soul is enriched with an abundance of every spiritual gift. . . . spiritual delight is tasted at its very source, and . . . we renew the memory of that surpassing love for us which Christ revealed in his passion.

It was to impress the vastness of this love more firmly upon the hearts of the faithful that our Lord instituted this sacrament at the Last Supper. . . . for those who were to experience the sorrow of his departure, it was destined to be a unique and abiding consolation. (From a work for the feast of Corpus Christi, quoted in ICEL, *Christian Prayer,* pp. 2011–2012)

Reflection

The celebration of the Eucharist is always a public act, so we must always appreciate its communal context. Even solitary adoration of the Blessed Sacrament is best seen in terms of its relation to the eucharistic celebration, in which the consecrated bread and wine are shared among the assembled members of the community. Historically, the eucharistic species began to be reserved so that it could be taken to those unable to join the assembly at worship because of sickness or some other serious reason.

The Eucharist, then, is not a private gift to be savored solely in one's heart; it is a sharing in Christ's animating power that ultimately expresses itself in greater love for neighbor. For Thomas as a Dominican preacher, the proclamatory power of the Eucharist was also critical. Participation in the Eucharist should lead us to a more radical manner of living, through which we promote the message of Christ by loving others.

✧ How does your reception of the Eucharist empower you to promulgate the Gospel of Jesus Christ? How is the Gospel more firmly planted in the world as a result of your participation in eucharistic worship?

✧ If you are able to, place yourself in the presence of the reserved sacrament. If this is not possible, choose a symbol for Christ such as a crucifix or a Bible open to the Gospels. Then, slowly and reverently, in much the same way you might employ a mantra, repeat the traditional prayer "O sacrament most holy, O sacrament divine, all praise and all thanksgiving be every moment thine!"

✧ Strategize ways that your participation at Sunday worship can become more communal. Perhaps this will mean introducing yourself to the person sitting next to you, or enjoying breakfast or brunch afterward with family members or friends with whom you attended the liturgy.

✧ The celebration of the Eucharist embraces a variety of experiences for the believer. In addition to being the Presence, it is also a commemoration, a sacrament of forgiveness, a celebration, a promise, a thanksgiving, a transforming message awaiting proclamation, and an expression of unity. Is this list complete? What else have you experienced through the Eucharist? List the fruits of the Eucharist in your life, and offer a prayer of thanksgiving for each.

✧ Mindful of the previous activity, enter into a dialogue with God over the following questions. Your engagement of each question could constitute its own prayer session.

✦ If the Eucharist is a commemoration, what does it recall, and how does that recollection affect your life today?
✦ If the Eucharist is a sacrament of forgiveness, for what are you asking forgiveness?
✦ If the Eucharist is a celebration, what is it celebrating?
✦ If the Eucharist is a promise, what does that promise mean for our world today? What does it mean for you personally?
✦ If the Eucharist is a thanksgiving, for what are you thankful?
✦ If the Eucharist is a transforming message awaiting proclamation, what changes in society or in your own life does it prescribe? What shape should the proclamation of this message take in your life?
✦ If the Eucharist is an expression of unity, with what are you united?

God's Word

For I received from the Lord what I also handed on to you, that the Lord Jesus on the night when he was betrayed took a loaf of bread, and when he had given thanks, he broke it and said, "This is my body that is for you. Do this in remembrance of me." In the same way he took the cup also, after supper, saying, "This cup is the new covenant in my blood. Do this, as often as you drink it, in remembrance of me." For as often as you eat this bread and drink the cup, you proclaim the Lord's death until he comes. (1 Corinthians 11:23–26)

Closing prayer:

Lord Jesus Christ,
you gave us the eucharist
as the memorial of your suffering and death.
May our worship of this sacrament of your body and blood
help us to experience the salvation you won for us
and the peace of the kingdom
where you live with the Father and the Holy Spirit,
one God, for ever and ever.

(ICEL, *Christian Prayer*, p. 656)

✧ Meditation 10 ✧

Petitionary Prayer

Theme: Aquinas understood petitionary prayer as the essence of prayer. Petitionary prayer helps us to image God as a loving parent who desires the best for us.

Opening prayer: Provident God, I desire to approach you with the confidence of a beloved child. You know my needs better than I know them myself. You are more aware of the needs of our suffering world than we could ever be. Help me to see your will in the events of my life and to grow in awareness of your divine will as I place my needs before you.

About Thomas

When the mendicant religious orders were still quite new, they attracted criticism regarding the degree to which their observances departed from the traditional norms associated with the religious life. Some outspoken critics charged that the mendicants could not be authentic religious because they did not observe a number of ascetic practices common to monastic life. In point of fact, the assiduous study to which the Dominicans were obliged could be achieved only by serious and practiced discipline. As time passed and as the Dominicans became more immediately associated with the intellectual life, their manner of approaching intellectual activity became a model for others.

It is in this respect that Thomas models the use and value of petitionary prayer. His workload was enormous. He was at his desk almost constantly, and his output was staggering. Nonetheless, he had his intellectual limits. At times, he could proceed no further with the task of clarifying and distinguishing the ways of God, and then he turned to prayer and fasting.

Acknowledging his dependence on God, Thomas would beseech God for clarification and understanding. He would petition God for assistance, and he would fast as a means of maintaining his attention on God. Ultimately, his prayer would be answered. Then, with a firmer grasp of the subject at hand, he would proceed with his theological work.

When confronted with his own limitations, even in the arena of his own specialization, Thomas humbly turned to God and asked for help. In his writings, he encouraged the faithful to always turn to God with their needs. Thomas noted that the prayer of petition is the foundation on which all other prayer is built. Those who habitually turn to the provident God with all their needs and believe that God takes delight in answering prayer, act very much in the spirit of Thomas Aquinas.

Pause: What do you ask of God today?

Thomas's Words

Divine providence does not merely arrange what effects are to occur; it also arranges the causes of these effects and the relationships between them. . . . in the case of prayer we do not pray in order to change God's plan, but in order to obtain by our prayers those things which God planned to bring about by means of prayers, in order, as Gregory says, that our prayers should entitle us to receive what almighty God planned from all eternity to give us. . . .

. . . We do not have to present our prayers to God in order to disclose to him our needs and desires, but in order to make ourselves realize that we need to have recourse to his help in these matters.

. . . Our prayer is not designed to change God's plan; the purpose of prayer is to obtain by our entreaties what God has already planned.

. . . God gives us many things out of sheer generosity, without being asked. The reason why he wants to give us some things in response to our petition is that it is profitable for us to acquire a certain confidence in running to him and to recognize that he is the source of all that is good for us. (Aquinas, *Summa* II-II, 83, 2, in Tugwell, p. 481)

Reflection

Thomas wrote that we grow in relationship with God simply by approaching God with our requests. In the moments that we faithfully confide our needs to God, we most typically tarry within the divine presence. Asking is conversation, and conversation in which God participates is always prayer. Of course, to mature and develop, all healthy relationships need to include more than a simple exchange of favors. Accordingly, the journey toward intimacy with God requires that prayer must also transcend the limits of presenting petitions. However, this does not deny the principle that God is always eager to hear our requests, and that in presenting requests, the petitioner is quite likely to grow in friendship with God and develop a sense of compassion for others.

✧ For Thomas, an essential aspect of asking for something was first making thanksgiving for the blessings already received from God. Consider the significant blessings you have received throughout your life, beginning with your early childhood. Perhaps it would be helpful to place them in a journal or on a notepad. Once you have brought those gifts to mind, make a prayer of thanksgiving to God for each of them. At another time, repeat this exercise, but bring to mind the rather ordinary gifts with which you have been blessed in the past few days. Make your prayer of thanksgiving for those.

✧ What does the suffering world most need today? Identify society's current needs and place them before God. Then ask yourself how God intends for *you* to be an aspect of the divine response to those needs. For example, if you have prayed for peace, how does God plan to use you as an agent of peace? How has God already responded to the needs of the world through you?

✧ Name the three things you most desire; identify anything you want. Now examine your desires. How closely do they parallel the values of Jesus Christ? What do your choices suggest about your spiritual life? Reflect on the last question. Does this reflection affirm your present value system or does it invite conversion? How will you respond to it?

✧ Pray for others. Situate yourself in a prayerful attitude with symbols of the people for whom you wish to pray (for example, a class roster or a family portrait). Pause over each individual, and ask God for whatever grace you feel that person most needs right now. Pray for someone who has hurt you. Ask God to grant them all they need in order to grow in holiness. Undoubtedly, this will be challenging; try your best. Then assess your feelings about the experience. Has God somehow blessed you through this prayer?

✧ Recall a time you asked God for something that you did not ultimately receive. What lesson was God trying to teach you by answering your petition in a manner that you neither anticipated nor desired? Can you understand that disappointing response as an expression of God's care and love for you?

God's Word

So I say to you, Ask, and it will be given you; search, and you will find; knock, and the door will be opened for you. For everyone who asks receives, and everyone who searches finds, and for everyone who knocks, the door will be opened. Is there anyone among you who, if your child asks for a fish, will give a snake instead of a fish? Or if the child asks for an egg, will give a scorpion? If you then, who are evil, know how to give good gifts to your children, how much more will the heavenly Father give the Holy Spirit to those who ask him! (Luke 11:9–13)

Closing prayer: Generous God, I believe that you answer all prayer. At times, your answer is difficult to recognize. At other times, your answer is obvious but baffling. Sometimes it seems that many of my prayers are not answered in the way that I had hoped, and I find myself losing confidence in the power of prayer. Help me always to turn to you in my need, and help me to grow in friendship with you as a result of those visits. Finally, help me to grow in my recognition of your loving presence in my life, regardless of your manner of answering my prayer. I ask this through Christ Jesus, the redeemer.

The Pater Noster

Theme: Aquinas directed much of his attention to the practical realities of Christian prayer. He focused on the need to attune one's will prayerfully to the will of God.

Opening prayer:

Our Father who art in heaven,
hallowed be thy name.
Thy kingdom come.
Thy will be done on earth, as it is in heaven.
Give us this day our daily bread,
and forgive us our trespasses,
 as we forgive those who trespass against us,
and lead us not into temptation,
but deliver us from evil.
Amen.

About Thomas

In 1273, within one year of his death, Thomas preached a series of Lenten sermons at the Church of San Domenico in Naples. Such preaching series were often part of the spiritual care local churches extended to their members. As his topic, Thomas chose to explain what he identified as the three greatest prayers: the Lord's Prayer, the Hail Mary, and the Apostles' Creed. In the course of the nearly sixty homilies in the series, Thomas progressed through each prayer until all three had been adequately interpreted.

The sermons were received with great enthusiasm by eager crowds. The popularity of these sermons reveals that in addition to being an extraordinary teacher and scholar, Thomas was also an eloquent preacher. He communicated as effectively with a congregation untrained in technical theological language as he did with his sophisticated colleagues and students in the academy. He integrated his academic expertise with his spirituality, and this wholesome integration manifested itself in pastoral preaching.

Thomas wrote that the Pater Noster (or Our Father, or Lord's Prayer; see the opening prayer for this meditation) is the best of all prayers, because it contains all five of the conditions he identified as necessary for prayer to be authentic. First, the Lord's Prayer must be prayed with *confidence,* by approaching God with complete security. Second, the Lord's Prayer must be prayed with *openness* to God's response to petitions, regardless of the answer. Third, the Lord's Prayer manifests the *order* required of proper prayer; in this prayer, Christ teaches his followers the proper hierarchy of values, to prefer the things of heaven over earthly concerns. Fourth, the Lord's Prayer teaches *devotion;* through this prayer, one sees that true devotion requires that one offer God love as well as charitable concern for neighbors. Finally, the Lord's Prayer leads one to *humility;* in this prayer, one learns not to rely on one's own resources but to rely on God alone.

In his ministry, Thomas led others in reflection on prayer, the Scriptures, philosophy, theology—the things of God. His preaching on the Lord's Prayer provides a concrete example of his habit of reflecting on something quite familiar in a way that led people to a new appreciation and greater depth of understanding. This is the gift of Thomas to the people of God.

Pause: Can you hear new meaning in each phrase of the Pater Noster each time you recite it?

Thomas's Words

We pray *Thy kingdom come* because the kingdom of heaven signifies the glory of paradise. . . .

. . . This kingdom is most desirable for three reasons:

a. Its supreme righteousness. It is desirable because of the supreme righteousness that obtains there: "Thy people shall be all righteous" [Isaiah 60:21]. Here below the wicked are mingled with the good, whereas in heaven there are no wicked and no sinners.

b. Its perfect liberty. This kingdom is desirable because of its perfect liberty. Although all men desire liberty naturally, here there is none; but in heaven there is perfect liberty without any trace of bondage: "The creature itself will be delivered from the slavery of corruption" [Romans 8:21].

In fact, not only will all be free, but all will be kings: "Thou hast made us to our God a kingdom" [Revelation 5:10]. This is because all shall be of one will with God: whatever the saints will, God shall will; and whatever God wills, the saints shall will. . . . In this way, all will reign, since the will of all will be done, and God shall be the crown of all. . . .

c. Its wondrous wealth. This kingdom is also desirable because of its wondrous wealth: "The eye hath not seen, O God, besides Thee, what things Thou hast prepared for them that wait on Thee" [Isaiah 64:4]. . . .

Take note that whatever man seeks in this world, he will find it more perfect and more excellent in God alone. If you seek delight, you will find supreme delight in God: "You shall see and your heart shall rejoice" [Isaiah 66:14]. . . . Do you seek wealth? You will find in Him all things you desire in abundance. (Aquinas, *Three Greatest Prayers*, pp. 125–127)

Reflection

Within the storehouse of Christian prayer is a treasury of well-known, formal prayers that each generation commits to memory and then passes on to the next age, and a parallel treasury of spontaneous, free-form prayers that arise from the human heart at a specific moment. Each constitutes an important piece of the Christian prayer tradition.

Free-form prayers subscribe to neither formula nor pattern and enable an intimately tailored encounter between God and the person at a specific moment, often with a particular need in mind. Formalized prayers, on the other hand, articulate some valuable aspect of Christian belief, and so contribute to the vital transmission of the faith from one generation to the next. The existence of familiar, formalized prayers also provides the community—which sometimes gathers from great distances and with a variety of cultural backgrounds—with a common language. People who have never before met can pray together in harmony as sisters and brothers.

It is a mistake to regard these two patterns of prayer as mutually exclusive and to treat a formal prayer such as the Lord's Prayer solely as community property with a usefulness limited to common prayer. Aquinas explains that the Pater Noster is the most excellent prayer and is therefore valuable for the solitary soul at prayer *and* for the worshiping community.

✧ Think ahead to the duties, activities, and encounters that will occupy you tomorrow. For each of those expected interactions, address the question, How can I engage this event with fidelity to the words "Thy kingdom come, / Thy will be done on earth, as it is in heaven"?

✧ Pray the Pater Noster slowly and intentionally, harvesting as much meaning as you can from each phrase. It may be helpful to gaze on the printed words of the text rather than pray it from memory.

✧ Rephrase the Lord's Prayer so that each part reflects something about your relationship with God as it is right now. For example: Replace the words "Our Father" with your own intimate way of addressing God. Replace the words "who art in heaven" with your own parallel description of God in glory. Replace "hallowed be thy name" with your own words of praise and blessing for God. Continue praying in this manner, individualizing every phrase according to your present circumstances. Write your prayer down, and change it as needed.

✧ In his *Three Greatest Prayers*, Thomas took each statement expressed in each prayer and expounded on the meaning behind its words. Approach the Pater Noster (or any other prayer you choose) in the same way: recite it phrase by phrase, and after each phrase, reflect on the deeper meaning the phrase expresses.

✧ Jesus taught us to address God as Father, but many today find this unsatisfactory. If you find the title *Father* to be wanting, there is no reason to force yourself to use it frequently. Yet, it is part of the tradition of our faith, and it could be valuable to attempt to appreciate it for communal or occasional personal use. Accordingly, reflect on the richness of meaning that can be communicated through this title when it is applied to God. Identify and acknowledge the causes of your difficulty with this name for God, and then note that it also possesses a number of positive features. What are they? Write them down. Make this a discussion between you and the first person of the Trinity, and regard it as prayer. The same exercise can also be worthwhile if you are completely comfortable addressing God as Father.

God's Word

He was praying in a certain place, and after he had finished, one of his disciples said to him, "Lord, teach us to pray, as John taught his disciples." He said to them, "When you pray, say:

Father, hallowed be your name.
  Your kingdom come.
  Give us each day our daily bread.
  And forgive us our sins,
      for we ourselves forgive everyone indebted
        to us.
  And do not bring us to the time of trial."

(Luke 11:1–4)

Closing prayer: Father in heaven, hear my prayer. I believe that communication with you helps to prevent me from offending your divine self, your people, and all of creation. I believe that communication provides me with an opportunity to petition you for your help, and to grow in knowing you by contemplating your responses to my requests. And most of all, I believe that communication with you strengthens our friendship. Help me, therefore, to follow your Son's teaching and remain always in constant communication with you, the source of my being.

Truth

Theme: Thomas Aquinas sought the truth in a great many sources. He dedicated his life to pursuing truth in order to explain the truths of God as well as he could.

Opening prayer: O Divine Truth, guide me toward an ever clearer understanding of you. Help me to be attentive when others speak of you; help me to see clearly when your ways are being explained; strip me of prejudice and bias so that I can be open to teachings about you that I find difficult; and most of all, let my pursuit of your truth lead me to a closer intimacy with you.

About Thomas

Thomas left no doubt about his passion for the truth and nothing but the truth. A legend recounts that on a typical day, Thomas was working in his study. At one point, some of the young friars in his priory, in a playful mood, knocked on Thomas's door. When he answered, they announced astonishing news. "Father Thomas," they chorused. "Quickly! Look out your window! An ox is flying across the sky!" Thomas immediately hurried to the window, opened it, and began searching the skies for the flying ox. Of course, this delighted his visitors no end, and after several moments, they doubled over in laughter. "It is a joke, Father Thomas; it is a joke! There is no ox in the sky!" they finally admitted, satisfied that their trick had succeeded. But Thomas would not let them have the last laugh. Instead of responding with a typical, "You got me," Thomas said, "I would prefer to believe that oxen have taken to flight than that my brothers would lie."

Some interpret this legend to suggest that Thomas was humorless; and indeed, some evidence suggests that at the very least, Thomas could be socially awkward. But their interpretation misses the larger point of the story: Thomas insisted that the truth be pursued seriously and unconditionally. Because the pursuit of truth leads to God, it was the unrivaled quest of his life.

Thomas beckons us to leave no stone unturned in seeking out the truth in all matters, for it is the presence of the Divine that will be found at the root of all truth.

Pause: How radically are you committed to the reign of truth?

Thomas's Words

The ultimate perfection of the human intellect is the truth of God. Other truths fulfil the intellect in view of the truth of God. (Aquinas, *Summa* II-II, 180, 4, in Tugwell, p. 550)

There are two ways in which things belong to the contemplative life: primarily or secondarily and preparatorily. What belongs to the contemplative life primarily is the contemplation of the truth of God, because it is this kind of contemplation which is the goal of human life as a whole. . . . but for the moment we are capable only of an imperfect contemplation of the truth of God, "in a mirror and obscurely" [1 Corinthians 13:12]. . . .

However, since we are led to the contemplation of God by way of his effects, in line with Romans 1:20, "The invisible things of God are seen in that they are understood by means of what he has made," the contemplation of God's effects is also a part of the contemplative life, but in a secondary role, namely that of leading us to the knowledge of God. So Augustine says that when we consider creatures we should not engage in an idle curiosity, which must sometime come to an end, we should make them a step toward the immortal realities which last forever. (Aquinas, *Summa* II-II, 180, 4, in Tugwell, pp. 548–549)

There are two ways in which people come to the knowledge of truth. One way is by means of what we receive from others. So with regard to what we receive from God prayer is necessary: "I called and the spirit of Wisdom came to me" [Wisdom 7:7]. With regard to what we receive from other people, listening is necessary . . . and reading is necessary. . . . The other way of coming to the knowledge of truth is by people undertaking their own study, and so meditation is needed. (Aquinas, *Summa* II-II, 180, 3, in Tugwell, pp. 546–547)

Reflection

Thomas's passion for truth led him to engage in dialogue with all sorts of wisdom sources. Constant conversation partners included the church fathers, commentators on the sacred Scriptures, and of course the holy Scriptures themselves. In an unprecedented way, Thomas also pursued the truth by engaging in philosophical dialogue with pre-Christian teachers such as the Greek philosophers Aristotle and Plato. Without betraying the truths and the heritage of his own Catholic Tradition, Thomas pushed the envelope of understanding further and further through his engagement of this wide variety of worthy sources, sometimes within the church and at other times outside it.

Changes in Thomas's opinions on selected issues over time indicate that he had adopted the dialogical approach to truth. Because he lived during a period when the church was often suspicious of new initiatives, his bold projects sometimes placed him in a vulnerable position. But his fidelity to the pursuit of truth resulted in great clarity of theological understanding for himself and immeasurable assistance to all

Christians who have benefited by his explanations about God and the things of God. Thomas witnesses to the wholesome pursuit of truth, which does not consist in the arrogant exclusion of other voices, but rather is the product of a genuine sharing of riches across confessional lines.

Today, in the tradition of Thomas, devout Christians also recognize other religions and philosophies as meaningful dialogue partners in the search for the truth that leads to God. The input of those partners is not to be viewed as a dilution of adherence to traditional Christian faith, but as an enhancement of the power of the Gospel to claim a person. When we have reflected on our faith in such a way that our presuppositions and beliefs are subject to comparison, challenge, and clarification, we emerge from the dialogue with a much firmer grasp of truth and with a mission to clarify remaining ambiguities. Accordingly, we come to understand that Thomas would not recognize contemporary Christians as coreligionists if they did not engage the faith questions of their time with earnestness and respect for differing voices.

✧ Call to mind the religious beliefs and convictions of people of other faiths. How do those "other voices" help you to know God better? Reflect on the contributions that other wisdom traditions offer to the human understanding of God and to the growth of goodness in the world, and make a prayer of thanksgiving for them. How can those contributions affect your life?

✧ Imagine the Christian community as being constructed of several different houses. Picture the Catholic edifice, the Protestant mansion, and the less well defined home of the unchurched believer. In addition, visualize another kind of Christian house: that of the nonbeliever who recognizes Jesus as the great teacher of authentic living. In this house, Jesus is not the Christ of faith, but a great teacher and philosopher who discovered the truth of the good life and conveyed it to others. It is not surprising that traditional Christians sometimes react strongly against including this house in the Christian community. Nonetheless, Jesus is the animating wisdom source for those in this house as well, and therefore his word has taken root in them.

Is it possible to imagine that some nonbelieving students of Jesus the Philosopher live the Gospel message even more radically than some believers? Enter into a mental conversation with a nonbeliever follower of Jesus, and try to understand Jesus, his teachings, and his role in the world, from a nonfaith perspective. Be attentive to what you can learn about Jesus from this exercise. What new insights into Jesus the Teacher can complement faith in Jesus the Christ? How might those insights draw you closer to Christ and to a more radical commitment to his teachings? How can reverent conversations about Jesus with nonbelievers enhance your own faith in him?

✧ What is truth? Compose a poem, or make a sketch or drawing, in which you symbolize the divine gift of truth and thank God for it.

✧ From time to time, a faithful Christian may experience difficulty understanding or accepting some aspect of the teachings of the faith. Such dilemmas can be confusing and painful, but often lead to deeper understanding. If you find yourself in such an episode, study the issue and discuss it with faith companions. Take the issue to God in prayer. Explain your struggle, give voice to your vulnerability, talk about the confusion and whatever other feelings you are experiencing, and place them before God. Listen patiently for the divine response. Always accompany your study and discussion with prayer such as this, so that your goal will be not victory over opposing points of view, but the pursuit of truth.

✧ Who are your wisdom sources? Who have shown you the path to truth in your life? Make a prayer of thanksgiving to God for those people. If they are still living, discern if it would be appropriate to communicate your sense of their gift to you. If they have died, consider writing them a letter, asking God to allow them to know of your sentiments. How do you continue to be faithful to the gifts of wisdom you have received?

God's Word

Jesus said to him, "I am the way, and the truth, and the life. No one comes to the Father except through me. If you know me, you will know my Father also. From now on you do know him and have seen him." (John 14:6–7)

Closing prayer: O God, to know you is to know delight. Help me to grow in my knowledge of your truth so that I will experience all the joys that you hold in store for those who know and love you.

✧ **Meditation 13** ✧

Study

Theme: As a member of the Dominican order, Thomas regarded study as a spiritual exercise. We emerge from dialogue with Thomas with a heightened awareness that study places us in the presence of the Holy.

Opening prayer: Creator God, our forebears in the faith have taught us that where your word is found, there also is found your work. When you uttered the words, "Let there be light," light came into existence! When you decreed, "Let there be life," at once life commenced! Help me to hear your word as I behold creation, the work of your hands. As I study created reality, help me to know that all this comes from you, and that the greater my understanding of creation, the greater the knowledge I will have of you, O Divine Creator.

About Thomas

When Thomas first entered the Dominican order in the early 1240s, the order was less than thirty years old. The Dominicans (like the Franciscans) represented a new way of life in the church; they were genuine religious, yet they moved beyond cloister walls. The appearance of this novel form of religious life surprised many people, perhaps mostly because the friars performed no daily manual farm labor.

Thirteenth-century Christians were simply unprepared to encounter religious whose day was not preoccupied with manual labor, just as they were unprepared to meet religious on the streets, outside of cloisters. This dual novelty describes the very reason that the mendicant form of religious life emerged. The church needed specialists who would carefully study the Scriptures and theology in order to move into the streets and the churches to deliver sound preaching. One cannot give what one does not possess, so one requires serious study as preparation for effective preaching. In fact, for the Dominicans, it was understood that study took the place of heavy manual labor and numerous other mortifications typical of religious of the day.

A Dominican, therefore, is a lifelong student, and Thomas is recognized as the ideal Dominican. For him, study was not merely a job; it was his passion. Study is not an end in itself; it is a discipline designed to bring us to greater wisdom and understanding of God and creation. The better we understand creation, the better we know the Creator; therefore, for Thomas, study was elevated to a form of worship of God.

Thomas once revealed the great value he invested in intellectual pursuit, while traveling on a religious pilgrimage with a group of fellow Dominicans. As they neared Paris, they reached an elevation that treated them to a splendid view of the great city. It was an awesome sight, which they enjoyed immensely. More than one of the friars remarked on its beauty with enthusiasm. Finally, one young friar tried to engage Thomas in the spirit of the moment by asking, "Thomas, wouldn't you like to be the master of that splendid city?" Thomas responded by asking his interrogator what would be the value in possessing the city. The friar suggested, "You could sell it and use the money it would earn to provide proper Dominican houses for all of our order's needs." To this, Thomas simply replied, "I would much sooner be in possession of Chrysostom's homilies on Matthew's Gospel."

Pause: Have you experienced study as a way of growing in intimacy with God?

Thomas's Words

Brother John, dear to me in Christ,

Since you have asked me how you ought to go about entering the treasury of knowledge, this is my advice to you:

I urge you to be slow to speak; slow to enter the visiting parlor.

Hold fast to purity of conscience.

Do not cease from devoting time to prayer. Love to frequent your own room if you desire to be led into the Lord's sanctuary of contemplation.

Show yourself to be amiable to everybody, or at least try to do so; but do not be overly familiar with anybody, for too much familiarity breeds contempt and introduces problems that impede study.

Also, do not get involved in the doings and sayings of other people that do not concern you. Above all, avoid aimless wandering about.

Do not heed by *whom* a thing is said; rather, *what* is wisely said you should commit to memory. Apply yourself to understanding what you read; verify what is doubtful. Strive to store whatever you can in the cupboard of your mind, as though you wanted to fill a vessel to the brim.

As the Scriptures say, "Seek not things that are too high for thee."

Follow in the footsteps of that blessed Dominic, who as long as he lived brought forth fruit in the vineyard of the Lord for the sake of his fellow travelers, fruit that was both practical and inspiring.

If you follow this advice, you will be able to attain what you desire. Farewell! (Adapted and paraphrased by Mary Mercy Houle, OP, from White, pp. 5–7)

Reflection

The Dominican ideal of study as a way of growing in intimacy with God is a gift that extends far beyond the confines of the order. Study is a natural way of growing in relationship with God. When we pursue a deeper understanding of the pages of the sacred Scriptures, we are engaging God's own Living Word. When we delve into the mysteries of theology, we become immersed in conversation that is about God's own self. When we examine any aspect of God's creation, we enhance the potential for gaining a deeper awareness of the author of all creation.

Remember that because God has caused all created reality to come into being, no field of study lies outside the boundaries of God's authorship or of God's care. The mathematician, the scientist, the poet, the economist, the political analyst, and the agriculturalist are concerned with God's creation just as are the priest, the nun, the spiritual director, the pastor, and the contemplative.

Also keep in mind that no theological work should be undertaken in a manner that separates it from the pastoral needs of the people of God. Thomas's great work the *Summa Theologiae* consists of reasonable objections followed by Thomas's responses. Thomas communicates an extremely important message through this choice of structure: he shows that study about the faith, the work of theology, must recognize the problems and questions of the day, and those must be dealt with in an honest fashion. Pondering the work of the Creator is a natural way of growing as a human being and in relationship with the Creator personally; theological study, therefore, possesses rich potential for spiritual growth.

✧ The next time you plan to study or read, prepare in this way (the subject to be studied makes no difference): Place yourself in your study position and tell God what you are about to study. Ask that you come to know God better through the study you are about to undertake. Ask the Holy Spirit to bless you with the discipline and understanding necessary to draw the greatest benefit from this period of work. Then study the material. Afterward, close your texts and converse with God for a few moments, discussing these items:

✦ How was this time that you and God spent together? What did you experience together?

✦ Make a prayer of thanksgiving for the handiwork of God with which you have just become better acquainted.

✦ How do you know God better as a result of this study period? How has your friendship with God grown as a result of your deeper understanding of created reality?

✧ Bring to mind a current controversial issue about which you have definite opinions. Write down your essential position on the topic. Next, ponder carefully, perhaps even reverently, statements and reflections of those who hold the opposite point of view. Can you learn anything new about this issue from your respectful listening? Can you begin to understand the values through which those who oppose you have come to their positions?

Do this exercise in the company of God, recalling that all people are created and loved by God. Even if your attitude remains unaltered or your own position is strengthened, this prayerful consideration of the issue will help you to grow in reverence for others by growing in recognition of the values they desire to protect. Even if you find that the opposing perspective is out of harmony with the Gospel and you reject it, your prayerful attentiveness to the dialogue will help you to regard the person who holds that position reverently, as Christ has commanded.

✧ Thomas noted that one danger of study is that people sometimes commit themselves to study that is less worthy than it could be. As an example, he pointed out some priests who neglected the study of the Scriptures in order to devote time to the enjoyment of stage plays.

Take a mental inventory of the kinds of issues to which you devote your free time. Ask yourself if, in addition to enjoying healthy recreational reading, you commit adequate and balanced study time to the following disciplines: the Scriptures, theology, political and current events, the international situation, the human sciences, the arts, and other topics to expand your horizons. Listen prayerfully for God's suggestions as to other disciplines that could be added to your list. Reflect on the value and beauty God has invested into all creation and areas of study, and on how each area of study can help you find your way into the divine presence. Conclude with a prayer of thanksgiving for all creation.

God's Word

Rejoice always, pray without ceasing, give thanks in all circumstances; for this is the will of God in Christ Jesus for you. Do not quench the Spirit. Do not despise the words of prophets, but test everything; hold fast to what is good; abstain from every form of evil. (1 Thessalonians 5:16–22)

Closing prayer:

Ineffable Creator,
    Who, from the treasures of Your wisdom,
        has established three hierarchies of angels,
        has arrayed them in marvelous order
            above the fiery heavens,
        and has marshaled the regions
            of the universe with such artful skill,

You are proclaimed
        the true font of light and wisdom,
        and the primal origin
            raised high beyond all things.

Pour forth a ray of Your brightness
        into the darkened places of my mind;
    disperse from my soul
        the twofold darkness
            into which I was born:
                sin and ignorance.

You make eloquent the tongues of infants.
        Refine my speech
        and pour forth upon my lips
            The goodness of Your blessing.
Grant to me
        keenness of mind,
        capacity to remember,
        skill in learning,
        subtlety to interpret,
        and eloquence in speech.

May You
        guide the beginning of my work,
        direct its progress,
        and bring it to completion.

You Who are true God and true Man,
        Who live and reign, world without end.

            Amen.

    (Aquinas, *Devoutly I Adore Thee*, pp. 41–43)

✦ Meditation 14 ✦

Preaching

Theme: Every baptized person, having been anointed as a prophet, is invited to contemplate the things of God, and to share the fruit of that contemplation with others; this is the most basic form of Christian preaching. Some are given specific responsibility for formal preaching, but all are called to witness to the Gospel by their lives.

Opening prayer: O God, source of all life, you have revealed yourself to humanity through your Living Word, your Son, Jesus Christ. The more I ponder your Word, the better I know you. My faith teaches me that as I grow to know you better, you expect me to share my experience of you with others. This sharing will take various forms and will occur in different places, but it is always a form of preaching, the ministry of the sharing of your Word. Speak to me and transform me so that all who come in contact with me will grow in friendship with you. Give me the grace to be a faithful proclaimer of your Living Word.

About Thomas

Thomas devoted his entire life to helping people to better understand God through preaching, teaching, and the written word. He was a master of theology, and as such had three major duties. The first two duties were carried out in the specialist environment of the academy: Thomas was expected to lecture students on the sacred Scriptures, and to engage in disputations, or public debates, with other academics who held contrary positions on particular topics. He excelled in both of these responsibilities.

Thomas's third duty was to preach. A master's preaching occurred in the university community typically, but not always, and Thomas preached in public churches as well.

It would be understandable if an academic master of theology were to preach above the heads of the typical parishioner, but Thomas did not. His preaching was pastoral and phenomenally popular with the lay public. In fact, some of Thomas's homilies, like the series he preached on the three greatest prayers near the end of his life, remain popular with Christians today. His gift for eloquently explaining God and the things of God to other people, whether sophisticated or simple, reveals that for him, his lifework of teaching and preaching was not simply a job, it was a vocation.

Pause: How do you proclaim the Gospel by your daily behavior?

Thomas's Words

The work of the active life is twofold. One proceeds from the fullness of contemplation, such as preaching and teaching. . . . And this is preferred to simple contemplation, for just as it is better to illumine than merely to shine, so it is better to give to others the things contemplated than simply to contemplate. The other work of the active life consists completely in exterior activity, such as almsgiving, reception of guests, and the like. And these are less excellent than the works of contemplation, except in case of necessity. . . .

Therefore religious institutes dedicated to preaching and teaching have the highest place. (Aquinas, *Summa* II-II, 188, 6)

Reflection

Many people quite understandably cringe when they hear the suggestion that they are called to be preachers of the Gospel. To begin with, the word *preach* has some negative connotations in our culture. We tend not to relish the idea of being "preached to," nor do we enjoy encountering someone who is "preachy." Many people resist the idea of preaching to others because they freeze at the thought of having to speak to an assembled group. Moreover, many Christians judge themselves to be inadequately prepared in theology or the Scriptures for preaching.

All these concerns are valid. Yet, Christian life is precisely a lifelong commitment to sharing the Good News of the Gospel with others. Gospel sharing occurs by word and by deed; it happens sometimes through eloquent and practiced oral delivery, sometimes through actions. Every instance of cooperation with God's Word, in any form, is a way of preaching, and preaching is the responsibility of every practicing Christian.

Thomas reminds us that the real issue behind our ability to preach is not so much style or venue as it is possessing God's Word and knowing God's ways through prayer, contemplation, and intimate exchange. The motto of the Dominican order is To contemplate and to share with others the fruits of our contemplation. Sharing the fruits of our contemplation is the essence of Christian preaching when we have been contemplating God's Word. One cannot share what one does not have; but the Christian has been given God's Word. Hence, listening to God's Word empowers us to share that Word with others. Ordained or not, engaged in professional ministry or not, we are empowered to share it with others. Thomas's lifelong friendship with God nurtured his ability to tell others about God. Following Thomas's example, people today find that in cultivating a life of prayer, they somehow become empowered to spread the Good News.

✧ Who has carried the Gospel to you? Recall the different virtues and lessons about God that you have learned since childhood from other people. In what ways has the "preaching" of other people drawn you closer to God? How are you being faithful today to those lessons in the faith? Prayerfully consider these things.

✧ If it is morning, look at the day ahead. If it is late in the day, focus on tomorrow. Ask God how you might go about sharing the Good News in the time ahead. What do you have to give to others? What treasure has God entrusted to you that you are expected to share? Thank God for this mission, and plan for how you will execute it.

✧ The goal of Christian preaching is to restore things to what they were like before the Fall, to build up the Reign of God. Honestly examine the ways you may have participated in tearing down the Reign. Make a prayer of contrition. Then balance this experience by recalling the ways that you have contributed to the building of God's Reign. Make a prayer of thanksgiving for those actions. Discuss with God your shared plans for your continued activity in the work of preparing for the fullness of the Reign of God.

✧ What is your favorite passage from the Scriptures? Commit it to memory. Memorizing God's word is a wonderful form of prayer. If you do not have a favorite Scripture passage, sit down with a Bible and scan the various books, chapters, and verses. Spend time with passages that lead you to reflect further. Ponder the meaning of the texts to which you are most drawn. Why do they seem appealing, attractive, or important to you? Engage God in a conversation about what God intends for you to learn through those texts. If you eventually discover one particular passage that speaks to you more than others, memorize it.

✧ Determine what the readings will be for your parish worship next Sunday. As a form of prayer, read those texts and reflect on them, trying to understand what God might be saying to you individually through them. Those who follow this prayer practice weekly are usually delighted to see how well it enhances their participation in the liturgy the following Sunday.

God's Word

[The Scriptures say,] "Everyone who calls on the name of the Lord shall be saved."

But how are they to call on one in whom they have not believed? And how are they to believe in one of whom they have never heard? And how are they to hear without someone to proclaim him? And how are they to proclaim him unless they are sent? As it is written, "How beautiful are the feet of those who bring good news!" (Romans 10:13–15)

Closing prayer: Living God, draw me to yourself. Speak to me through your Divine Word, so that I can know you better in order to proclaim you better. Let my every action be done in accord with your Holy Word, so that my life is a constant proclamation that Jesus Christ is Lord.

✧　**Meditation 15**　✧

"Nothing but You, O Lord!"

Theme: The greatest of life's treasures is the Lord Jesus Christ.

Opening prayer: Christ Jesus, beloved friend, I have been blessed in this life with many gifts and treasures, but none is so precious as my relationship with God, which I possess only through you. Instill within me an ever-growing desire for you, a desire that will result in more profound intimacy with the Triune God. Amen.

About Thomas

Thomas practiced a daily custom of praying in the chapel in the early morning hours before the rest of the community assembled for liturgical prayer. While he was assigned to the Priory of San Domenico in Naples, he would have prayed in the Chapel of Saint Nicholas. During this period, Thomas was writing the third part of the *Summa Theologiae*, which treats subjects grouped under the heading "Christ, the Way to Eternal Life."

Thomas's pattern of solitary early morning prayer apparently aroused the curiosity of Brother Dominic of Caserta, who, as sacristan, was responsible for the care of the altar and the community's worship space. Determined to witness what occurred during Thomas's prayer sessions, early one morning, the sacristan concealed himself in the chapel.

Brother Dominic reported that first he saw Thomas praying wholeheartedly before the crucifix. After a certain period of time, Thomas was apparently transported by the intensity of his prayer and actually rose up a few feet into the air. While Thomas maintained this attitude of prayer, the figure of Christ on the cross said: "You have written well of me, Thomas. What reward would you have for your efforts?" Thomas replied simply and spontaneously, "Nothing but you, O Lord!"

Pause: What desires stand in the way of your wanting or desiring God with all your heart?

Thomas's Words

O merciful God, may I rejoice in nothing except what leads to you, nor be saddened except by what leads away from you.

May I not seek to please anyone, or fear to displease anyone, except you.

May all transitory things seem worthless to me, O Lord, and eternal things seem dear to me.

May every joy without you weary me, and may I desire nothing besides you.

May work done for you, O Lord, delight me; and may all repose without you be wearisome to me.

Grant, O my God, that I direct my heart to you, and in failure grieve constantly with the purpose to amend. . . .

Give me, O Lord God, an ever watchful heart, which no overcurious speculation may lead away from you; a noble heart, which no unworthy affection may draw downward; a right heart, which no wrong intention may turn aside; a firm heart, which no tribulation may break; a free heart, which no vehement affection may claim.

Bestow on me, O Lord, my God, a mind that knows you, a diligence that seeks you, a wisdom that finds you, a manner of acting that pleases you, a perseverance that confidently awaits you, a trust that finally embraces you.

Grant that I may . . . make use of your favors on the way, through grace, and possess perfectly your joys in heaven. . . . Amen. (Adapted by Mary Mercy Houle, OP, from Curia Generalizia OP, p. 328)

Reflection

When Thomas responded that he wanted "nothing but you, O Lord," he announced the passion of his heart and the purpose of his life. His entire life and his voluminous theological work are best represented by this simple yet exquisitely profound expression of desire for union with the Divine.

This story about Thomas teaches us about the Christian faith as certainly as any of his lectures or theological writings do. The same refrain, "Nothing but you, O Lord," expresses the goal and desire of the contemporary Christian.

✧ Create whatever kind of environment most helps you to pray, and then place yourself in a meditative posture. Over and over, use the following words as a mantra: "I want nothing but you, O Lord."

✧ Place yourself in the presence of a crucifix. Hear Christ promising you that he will fulfill any desire you choose. Name your desires. Listen to those desires as you express them. Reflect on what your choices tell you about your values and your relationships with Christ and with others.

✧ Imagine that you live in the time of Jesus, and that you know him. Are you a friend of Jesus'? Do you like him? Do you want to follow him? What things about his human nature do you like? What draws you to him?

✧ What name for Christ best suits your relationship with him? Call him by that name. What name for you does Christ use when you are at prayer? What do the names that you and Christ use for each other reveal about the dynamics and the level of intimacy that occur between the two of you?

✧ Pray the following litany to Christ. After calling on Christ using the various names and titles in the litany, continue by addressing Christ with various names and titles that emerge from your relationship with the Lord.

> Jesus, model of all virtue; I want nothing but you, O Lord.
> Jesus, the compassion of God; I want nothing but you, O Lord.
> Jesus, word of God; I want nothing but you, O Lord.
> Jesus, the way, the truth, and the life; I want nothing but you, O Lord.
> Christ Crucified; I want nothing but you, O Lord.
> Body of Christ; I want nothing but you, O Lord.

Liberator Christ; I want nothing but you, O Lord.
Christ, my beloved; I want nothing but you, O Lord.
Christ, teacher of faith; I want nothing but you, O Lord.
Christ, promise of hope; I want nothing but you, O Lord.
Christ, living charity; I want nothing but you, O Lord.
Christ, counselor of prudence; I want nothing but you, O
Lord.
Christ, the just one; I want nothing but you, O Lord.

God's Word

Jesus asked the twelve, "Do you also wish to go away?"
Simon Peter answered him, "Lord, to whom can we go?
You have the words of eternal life. We have come to believe and know that you are the Holy One of God." (John
6:67–69)

Closing prayer: Christ Jesus, instill within me a desire for
you above all other desires, so that with Thomas Aquinas, I
too will pray, "I want nothing but you, O Lord!"

WISDOM

✧ Works Cited ✧

Aquinas, Thomas. *Commentary on the Gospel of John, Chapter 14.* Quoted in *Saint Thomas Aquinas: Meditations for Every Day*, trans. E. C. McEniry. Columbus, OH: Long's College Book Company, 1951.

———. *Devoutly I Adore Thee: The Prayers and Hymns of St. Thomas Aquinas.* Trans. and ed. Robert Anderson and Johann Moser. Manchester, NH: Sophia Institute Press, 1993.

———. *Summa Theologiae.* [Cambridge?, Eng.]: Blackfriars; New York: McGraw-Hill, 1964–1975.

———. *The Three Greatest Prayers: Commentaries on the Lord's Prayer, the Hail Mary, and the Apostles' Creed.* Trans. and rev. Sophia Institute Press. Manchester, NH: Sophia Institute Press, 1990.

———. *The Ways of God.* Manchester, NH: Sophia Institute Press, 1995.

Catholic Book Publishing Company. *Lectionary for Mass.* New York: Catholic Book Publishing Company, 1970.

Curia Generalizia OP. *Dominican Prayer Book.* 4th and rev. ed. Rome: Curia Generalizia OP, 1962.

International Commission on English in the Liturgy (ICEL), preparers of English translation. *Christian Prayer: The Liturgy of the Hours.* New York: Catholic Book Publishing Company, 1976.

———. *The Sacramentary.* New York: Catholic Book Publishing Company, 1985.

John Paul II. *Faith and Reason* (*Fides et Ratio*, 15 October 1998). As quoted in *Origins*, vol. 28, no. 19, 22 October 1998, p. 330.

Libreria Editrice Vaticana. *Catechism of the Catholic Church.* Trans. United States Catholic Conference (USCC). Washington, DC: USCC, 1994.

O'Meara, Thomas Franklin. *Thomas Aquinas: Theologian.* Notre Dame, IN: University of Notre Dame Press, 1997.

Torrell, Jean-Pierre. *Saint Thomas Aquinas.* Vol. 1, *The Person and His Work.* Trans. Robert Royal. Washington, DC: Catholic University of America Press, 1996.

Tugwell, Simon, trans. and ed. *Albert and Thomas: Selected Writings.* Mahwah, NY: Paulist Press, 1988.

Weisheipl, James A. *Friar Thomas D'Aquino: His Life, Thought, and Work.* Garden City, NY: Doubleday and Company, 1974.

White, Victor. *How to Study.* 6th ed. London: Blackfriars Publications, 1956.

✧ For Further Reading ✧

Barron, Robert. *Thomas Aquinas: Spiritual Master*. New York: Crossroad Publishing Company, Spiritual Legacy Books, 1996.

Davies, Brian. *The Thought of Thomas Aquinas*. Oxford: Clarendon Press, 1992.

Fatula, Mary Ann. *Thomas Aquinas: Preacher and Friend*. Collegeville, MN: Liturgical Press (Michael Glazier), 1993.

Wadell, Paul. *The Primacy of Love: An Introduction to the Ethics of Thomas Aquinas*. New York: Paulist Press, 1992.

Acknowledgments *(continued)*

The scriptural quotations in this book are from the New Revised Standard Version of the Bible. Copyright © 1989 by the Division of Christian Education of the National Council of the Churches of Christ in the United States of America. All rights reserved.

Permission has been requested to use the quotes herein from *Summa Theologiae,* by Thomas Aquinas.

The quotes herein from *Albert and Thomas: Selected Writings,* translated and edited by Simon Tugwell, OP, are used with permission of the publisher. Copyright © 1988 by Simon Tugwell, OP.

Permission has been requested to use the liturgical adaptation of Daniel 3:57–88 on pages 41–42, from *Christian Prayer: The Liturgy of the Hours,* English translation prepared by the International Commission on English in the Liturgy (ICEL).

All other quotes herein from *Christian Prayer* are used with permission from ICEL. Copyright © 1974, ICEL. All rights reserved.

The Apostles' Creed on pages 42–43 is quoted from, the opening prayer on page 73 is adapted from, and the memorial acclamation on page 81 is quoted from *The Sacramentary,* English translation prepared by the ICEL, pages 369, 272, and 545, respectively.

The quotes herein from *Devoutly I Adore Thee: The Prayers and Hymns of St. Thomas Aquinas,* by Thomas Aquinas, are used with permission of the publisher. Copyright © 1993 by Robert Anderson and Johann Moser.

The quote herein from *The Ways of God,* by Thomas Aquinas, is used with permission. Copyright © 1995 by Sophia Institute.

The opening prayer on page 90 is quoted from the *Catechism of the Catholic Church,* by the Libreria Editrice Vaticana, number 2759.

The quote herein from *The Three Greatest Prayers: Commentaries on the Lord's Prayer, the Hail Mary, and the Apostles' Creed,* by Thomas Aquinas, is used with permission. Copyright © 1990 by Sophia Institute.

Titles in the Companions for the Journey Series

Praying with Anthony of Padua
Praying with Benedict
Praying with C. S. Lewis
Praying with Catherine McAuley
Praying with Catherine of Siena
Praying with Clare of Assisi
Praying with the Celtic Saints
Praying with Dominic
Praying with Dorothy Day
Praying with Elizabeth Seton
Praying with Francis of Assisi
Praying with Francis de Sales
Praying with Frédéric Ozanam
Praying with Hildegard of Bingen
Praying with Ignatius of Loyola
Praying with John Baptist de La Salle
Praying with John Cardinal Newman
Praying with John of the Cross
Praying with Julian of Norwich
Praying with Louise de Marillac
Praying with Martin Luther
Praying with Meister Eckhart
Praying with Pope John XXIII
Praying with Teresa of Ávila
Praying with Thérèse of Lisieux
Praying with Thomas Aquinas
Praying with Thomas Merton
Praying with Vincent de Paul

Order from your local religious bookstore or from

Saint Mary's Press
702 TERRACE HEIGHTS
WINONA MN 55987-1320
USA
1-800-533-8095